I Used to Think . . . And Now I Think . . .

I Used to Think . . . And Now I Think . . .

—ɰ—

Twenty Leading Educators Reflect on the Work of School Reform

Edited by
RICHARD F. ELMORE

Harvard Education Press
Cambridge, Massachusetts

HARVARD EDUCATION LETTER
IMPACT SERIES

Chapter 5, by Richard F. Elmore, originally appeared as "I Used to Think . . . and Now I Think . . ." in the January/February 2000 issue of the *Harvard Education Letter*.

Chapter 6, by Howard Gardner, originally appeared in the September/October issue of the *Harvard Education Letter*.

Library of Congress Control Number 2010942142

Paperback ISBN 978-1-934742-85-3
Library Edition ISBN 978-1-934742-86-0

Published by Harvard Education Press,
an imprint of the Harvard Education Publishing Group

Harvard Education Press
8 Story Street
Cambridge, MA 02138

Cover Design: Sarah Henderson
The typefaces used in this book are Apollo and Type Embellishments

Contents

Introduction

—⟪w⟫—

Richard F. Elmore

S even or eight years ago, I began to conclude my courses and professional development sessions with a simple protocol called *I used to think . . . , and now I think . . .* It consists of asking students to complete a two-column exercise. One column says "I used to think . . . ," which captures key ideas and preconceptions they had when they entered the course or session, and another, "and now I think . . . ," which captures their thoughts on the same subject after the course or session. We usually follow these individual reflections with a Quaker-style session in which people speak about their reflections when they choose to, with no obligation for anyone to speak. This protocol originated with the very useful Web site Visible Thinking, sponsored by Harvard Project Zero, which contains a number of ideas for how teachers can encourage students to talk about their learning and, in doing so, build more powerful disciplines of thought.[1]

I don't know exactly why I originally adopted this protocol— I have a habit of experimentation in the classroom that, as my students will testify, doesn't always lead to good results. I do, however, remember that I regarded it as risky. After all, what would happen if students said that the experience had no impact at all on their thinking? I remember very clearly being stunned and surprised by what I heard—as I continue to be every time

1

I use the protocol. What I find most striking about students' reflections is not how closely they capture what I thought I was teaching—which is often enough the case to keep me going—but the multiple meanings they make of their learning. The experience is enough to forever disabuse one of the simple connection between what is taught and what is learned.

Then, about a year ago, I wrote a short piece for the *Harvard Education Letter* about how my own thinking had changed over the course of the forty years or so I had been teaching and doing research in the education sector.[2] It was that piece that stimulated this book. The essays in this volume are, I think, testimonials to the broader value of this simple, reflective protocol. I asked the authors for short reflections in response to the protocol; they have been courageous in their willingness to take this risk and have produced work that models reflective practice.

Currently, we live in a political, social, intellectual, and cultural environment that seems to value hard ideological boundaries and fixed truths, as if the world were arrayed into irreconcilable factions, arguing from hard premises to predetermined conclusions. Perhaps this climate stems from a sense of danger in the uncertainty and flux that surrounds us. But uncertain times, one could just as well argue, require flexibility, reflectiveness, and agility of mind—qualities of disciplined learning.

The purpose of bringing these articles together is, in the words of the original Project Zero protocol, to make learning visible—in this case, over the course of the careers of leading educators. In doing so, my fellow contributors and I hope to model, in a small way, what professional discourse might look like if professionals were expected to learn over the course of a career, to develop a more complex and variegated mind-set, and, sometimes, to change what they think in some fundamental way. It strikes me as ironic that in a field nominally devoted to the development of capacities to learn, there is so little visible evidence of what those who do the work have actually learned in their careers.

This book, then, is an invitation to join in a broader professional discourse, to join in a community of reflective practice that values growth and development disciplined by logic and evidence. Try this yourself, and try it with your colleagues.

1

ARGUING FOR THEORY

—ɯ—

Jean Anyon

I have been arguing for theory in educational research since 1982. That year, in an article in the journal *Theory into Practice*, I made the case that our research should employ theory that is empirically situated, theoretically explanatory, and socially critical.[1] By *empirically situated* I meant that one collects data at a micro level and uses it to build a theory of society; by *socially critical* I meant to return to the classical notion of *theoria* as *phronesis*—a practical guide to understanding. Such practical understanding could be arrived at by linking micro data and macro theories.[2]

Twelve years later, in the pages of *Curriculum Inquiry*, I argued more explicitly that educational scholars should develop theoretical approaches that will be of real help in the fight for a better world.[3] Toward "socially useful theory" I argued again that, in addition to several politically motivated criteria, research should connect micro and macro spheres:

Categories of a socially useful theory . . . result from a dialogue between concepts of one's goal or vision, and people's current

5

activities and problems . . . Useful theory would be neither total (and therefore seamless and deterministic) nor completely ad hoc and applicable to only one locale. Rather, it would acknowledge the complex narratives that connect larger social structures and daily life, and would seek theories that connect local activity to widespread societal constraints . . . A penultimate characteristic of socially useful theory is that the theoretical recommendations put forward must be capable of enactment. Moreover, these recommendations should embody the values and ultimate goals of the theory . . . For example, a theory that urges, as does Marxism, the end of oppression, must not oppress others . . . Finally, a theory that would be useful in changing society will identify direct actions to be taken. Useful theory will have as a primary goal not the refinement of concepts, but successful political activity.[4]

These criteria were robust and fairly explicit. There was only one problem. My own work did not fulfill the requirements. My scholarship applied the tenet that theory should be critical and should link one's political concerns to empirical work, and one's theoretically grounded recommendations ought to be capable of enactment. But there were no people in my research, there was no narrative of daily life, there was no micro. The use of structural Marxism (in my early studies of social class and school knowledge) and then political economy (in *Ghetto Schooling* and my most recent *Harvard Educational Review* article) produced important knowledge about the relation of the economic system to education, but these works provided little, if any, understanding of micro situations—of cultural meaning-making or individual agency.[5] My theory was not capable of capturing these, and so I could not completely account for or explain what I saw. The contradiction I faced while preparing those pieces was that I did not want to excise culture and individual meaning-making from the research I carried out, yet I was not able *politically* to give up the insights into an unequal system that I believed a class-based, macro perspective afforded me. I had no socially critical theory that I felt would successfully link macro and micro together.

After teaching undergraduates for twenty years, I joined a doctoral program in urban education in 2001. I soon noticed that most of my students knew very little theory—Marxist or otherwise. I myself had kept up with various theoretical developments in social science over the years but had not read extensively outside the theoretical Left of Marx, Habermas, Althusser, David Harvey, Saskia Sassen, Frederick Jameson, and such. To prepare for the theory courses I wanted to teach, I undertook deep readings of scholars like Michel Foucault, Judith Butler, Pierre Bourdieu, Arjun Appadurai, Saba Mahmood, Nancy Fraser, Michael Dawson, and James C. Scott. As I read, I realized that these theorists suggested ways to look inside systems and structures for the people and cultures that populate and create them. My 2005 book, *Radical Possibilities*, attempted a partial resolution of my conflict, as it reconstructed received social movement theory to put personal and group agency center stage as movers of history via political contestation and social movements.[6]

I have been led, by these readings and by working with doctoral students, to ponder how my earlier research might have differed had I been more attentive to the micro world of

> *My scholarship applied the tenet that one's theoretically grounded recommendations ought to be capable of enactment. But there were no people in my research, there was no narrative of daily life, there was no micro.*

informants. What would these earlier studies have revealed if I had documented informants' lay theories about the macro forces they encountered and had to negotiate? Might I—calling on Anthony Giddens's work perhaps—have discovered in my 1980s study of social class and school knowledge the *reciprocity* of production and reproduction, showing, for example, the agency of teachers and students in cocreating and perhaps resisting the economic determinations of a school's social context?[7] Might I in *Ghetto Schooling*—alerted to disguised cultural critique as described by James C. Scott—have been able to penetrate the public transcripts of policy to understand how educators and families in Newark, New Jersey, pushed back and resisted the system that oppressed them?[8] Or—in the language of Michel Foucault—might I have perceived ways students and families refused to be normalized (victimized) by the gathering forces of ghettoization?[9] Had I been able to weave these micro theoretical analyses into my exposition of macro structures, such research could have produced richer data and fuller explanations of events than the reports I published. By portraying the instantiation of micro and macro processes in and with each other, I would have connected culture and political economy, agency and structure; I would have provided a fuller picture of social production, reproduction, and the development of urban political economy. However, I did not see the need for new theory at the time, and therefore did not look for the theoretical tools to attempt this larger agenda.

But after teaching Foucault for several years, I realized his theory was seriously challenging my Marx-inspired conception of social *power*. Power, I began to understand, does not only "descend" from the state or the corporate and political elites; it is, as Foucault alleged, the air we breathe. We produce power and are produced by it.[10] Foucault's conceptual arsenal seemed clearly capable of undermining my structural Marxism. I have since been searching for a vocabulary that will allow me to connect the two.

Pedagogical work with students—and my own search for theories that capture both social structure and personal agency—evolved into a 2009 book that recounts and models the processes my students and I developed to expand the role theory can play in educational research.[11] We see theory entering the research process everywhere—in posing empirical questions, in deciding what counts as data, and in analysis and explanation. I wrote an overview for the book of what theory is and can be, what it can do, and why it is necessary. Each of the substantive chapters by a former doctoral student describes how she used theory—and sometimes how theory used her—before and during dissertation work. As I watch my students use theory with growing sophistication and skill, I feel that I have learned more from them than they from me.

> *I have been led, by these readings and by working with doctoral students, to ponder how my earlier research might have differed had I been more attentive to the micro world of informants.*

For example, as I worked with one student, a community organizer, on her chapter for our theory book, I observed how she used the theories of Pierre Bourdieu to sharpen the advocacy skills of a group of low-income Latina parents. These women were attempting to negotiate for their children the complex high school choice process in the New York City district. As they learned about Bourdieu's concepts of cultural and social capital, and the power of dominant modes of speaking, dressing, and forming political ties, they saw ways to improve their practice. Bourdieu's theories offered them a language to put into practice knowledge they may have intuited but had not formalized for use. My student's project showed me how macro theory can be useful on the ground.

The process of "kneading" the theory/research/data mix in the years I have belonged to a doctoral faculty is exciting. It has catalyzed in me a new sense of intellectual agency. The search itself is invigorating.

2

METIS AND THE METRICS
OF SUCCESS

—ɷ—

Ernesto J. Cortés Jr.

I used to think a lot of things. I used to think tests were use-ful tools because they were diagnostic; now I think that the testing regime is crippling our public schools because it makes tests punitive. I used to think that if we amassed enough evidence of our success in reorganizing the culture of schools in collaboration with other community institutions that superintendents would let us have genuine local governance and control, that our schools would in effect be able to function as subdistricts within the larger system. Now I think that the fear generated by the punitive, top-down, standardized testing system virtually eliminates that possibility. I used to think that the evidence of our success would attract attention and lead to genuine change in thinking about school reform; now I think that if the evidence comes out of people's experience and local knowledge instead of from data analyzed by experts, it just gets ignored.

Evidence is important. I would never suggest otherwise. Data is important, but data is not the only kind of evidence. Data is abstract and easily manipulated. It has even been said that while numbers don't lie, liars do use numbers. Data is useful only to the extent that it reflects reality and its users have a clear understanding of its limitations. The all-too-frequent "suggestion" that we need to further "drill down" into the data that come from standardized tests ignores the fact that our testing system is deeply flawed. The notion of standardized tests as a single measure is by its very nature ridiculous, because it suggests that there are standardized kids with standardized brains.

Education and learning cannot be measured and evaluated in the same way that profits are counted and production is managed—a fact that far too many leaders of the business and philanthropic communities fail to understand. Standardized tests and resulting data are one way to measure the success of our schools, but, taken out of context, they lose much of their meaning. Nor is it in the real interest of teaching and learning for districts to be run by charismatic individuals who see themselves as CEOs at one stop on their ladders to greatness rather than as leaders of communities of learners. Superintendents best serve their districts when they engage the people in the school community—teachers, parents, and community leaders—who have what the Greeks called *metis,* or local knowledge. Metis emerges from experience and is embedded in practice.

Frequently people don't even realize their own expertise until they start having conversations with one another about their work. Classroom teachers, for example, are often so busy doing the teaching that they are not aware of their own learning, which is embedded in their practice and habits. People must be encouraged, guided, and mentored to reflect on what they learn from their experiences. It is through such structured and focused conversations, both between individuals and within small groups, that the local knowledge is recognized and articulated. It is through the kinds of above experiences that what we call *social knowledge* is both contextualized and understood.

Superintendents best serve their districts when they engage the people in the school community— teachers, parents, and community leaders—who have what the Greeks called metis, or local knowledge.

Now, as James C. Scott reminds us in his book *Seeing Like a State*, the litmus test for metis is practical success.[1] Or, in the context of school reform, is real learning taking place?

For many years our community organizing work with a network of public schools throughout Texas (the Alliance Schools Project) generated greater improvements on standardized tests than those experienced by schools of similar socioeconomic status. Our schools also experienced increases in attendance and improved morale among staff. The development of teachers as leaders in our schools led them to become teachers of educators as well as of students. Many became principals who viewed themselves as head teachers and mentors rather than administrators. As head teachers, their job was to create communities of learners, which focused on caring adults who felt responsible and committed to the development of young people. Building that community involved working with an organizer to identify leadership potential among parents, teachers, classified workers, and members of other neighborhood institutions (churches, synagogues, mosques, temples) who were willing to strategize and work together to build a culture of genuine teaching and learning. The development of parents as leaders meant that they shared in the guidance of the school community, influencing everything from the availability of health services to making the curricula more challenging to students. The engagement of neighborhood institutions in the life of the school meant that bonds were passed and facilities were upgraded.

The development of the adults in and around the school community dramatically affected the ability of students to learn but was very difficult to quantify. The experts couldn't subject it to regression analysis, and in the face of policies like the No Child Left Behind Act, it became difficult to sustain on a large scale. At the same time, many of the foundations that had supported our work started looking for something new and different to try.

However, one of the foundations that continued to support the school organizing decided to also invest resources in a serious evaluation of the work of Austin Interfaith. Researchers posed three questions: In what ways has Austin Interfaith's organizing influenced school district policy? To what degree has Austin Interfaith's organizing influenced the capacity of schools to educate students successfully? Has Austin Interfaith's organizing produced measurable gains in student outcomes?

The results of their study, including a regression analysis of the relationship between Austin Interfaith's involvement and student performance on Texas's standardized test, were overwhelmingly positive. Deep involvement of Austin Interfaith in a campus predicted gains in standardized test scores ranging from fifteen to nineteen points, while more peripheral engagement led to only four points of improvement.[2] The study also documented that some of the benefits of Austin Interfaith's organizing efforts spilled beyond the campuses directly involved with the organization to extend to all low-income campuses in the district.

Were there trumpets? Heralds of a new era in school reform? Even widespread press coverage? Not so much.

Now, to be fair, a number of thoughtful researchers in the field of education have examined our work with schools over the years. Howard Gardner, Richard Murnane, Dennis Shirley, Thomas Hatch, and others have spoken and written eloquently about the successes of the Alliance Schools. Unfortunately, it is difficult to be heard above the drumbeats of charter schools, performance-based pay, prescribed curricula, and the like.

Part of the difficulty is that our strategy takes time, or what we refer to as *patient capital*. It takes time to develop leaders, to develop relationships, to develop the social knowledge necessary to understand what we know and what we are learning. It takes time to develop trust. In his book *So Much Reform, So Little Change*, Charles Payne cites a lack of trust among adults as creating dysfunction in schools. In schools where trust among adults is built over time, Payne says, student achievement improves.[3] This certainly mirrors our experience with the Alliance Schools.

> *Part of the difficulty is that our strategy takes time, or what we refer to as* patient capital. *It takes time to develop leaders, to develop relationships, to develop trust.*

It takes time to develop a culture of constant learning, one that includes not only students but also the adults in a school community. At its best, our organizing leads to a culture that continues to evolve rather than one that is rigid, fixed, or proscribed. Part of the challenge is that many people are looking for a one-size-fits-all model for school reform. Yet schools exist in different contexts and different situations, and those contexts and situations change over time.

This may be another part of the difficulty in recognizing the value of the work: in our strategy, school "reform" is never finished. Constant evaluation and adaptation is required. Why? Because conditions change. Populations shift. Technologies emerge. Facilities deteriorate. Resources come and go. Economies falter. Families come under different kinds of pressures all the time—and those are the same families who are sending their children to the school. They are the same families whose adults are the parents, the teachers, and the classified workers at the school.

Circumstances alter, and unless the culture of a school is one of ongoing learning and adaptation, one that constantly supports the development of new leaders, then the ability to respond to new and different stimuli is lost.

The notion that it is a good idea for a superintendent to know at 10:00 a.m. what page every fourth-grade teacher in his or her district is teaching from is ridiculous. The factory model of education has been discredited repeatedly over the last decades. Even if the primary purpose of an education was to prepare students for employment (which it is not), the factory model does a disservice to young people preparing for the twenty-first-century economy. In a top-down culture that reinforces passivity—in both students and adults—no one is learning to be creative and initiatory. No one is learning what Frank Levy and Richard Murnane described as the soft skills: the ability to communicate effectively both orally and in writing, the ability to solve problems by forming and testing hypotheses, the ability to work well with persons from different backgrounds. No one is learning what the leaders of Motorola described as the "most critical skill" in their introduction to Levy and

Murnane's *Teaching the New Basic Skills*—the ability to learn and keep learning, to become lifelong learners.[4]

Lifelong learning is predicated on the understanding that intellectual capital is more than merely information; it is the ability to analyze and reflect. We have to be prepared to teach students the wonder, awe, and beauty of the U.S. Constitution while also recognizing it as a deeply flawed document that ignored women, men without property, and the horrors of slavery. Teaching (as opposed to mere instruction) should transmit the value of and appreciation for a democratic culture while at the same time prepare students to challenge it and to learn from its shortcomings.

In fact, the primary reason taxpayers should support public education is because of the way in which it (ideally) inculcates the vision and values of a democratic culture. Only if education is about teaching people—particularly young people—to understand other perspectives and points of view while maintaining the ability to debate and argue their own can we hope to sustain democracy in the face of the growing isolationism, cynicism, and polarization not just in our own nation but in the global community.

Even for adults, the public schools are a source of democratic participation. In her book *The Death and Life of the Great American School System*, Diane Ravitch cites neighborhood schools as the only local institutions "where people congregate and mobilize to solve local problems, where individuals learn to speak up and debate and engage in democratic give-and-take with their neighbors."[5]

Watching the Senate Judiciary Committee during the confirmation hearings for Elena Kagan, I was struck by how truncated our concept of debate has become and by our inability to engage in anything other than station identification. By this I mean our tendency to basically identify ourselves and our predetermined positions, then (at best) pause appropriately while someone else speaks and we think about what we are going to say next. It is as if we have lost the capacity for genuine engagement, contestation, and argument—the kind of debate that leads to some sort of negotiated settlement and compromise. More than ever today, we need institutions to teach these kinds of habits and practices that are central to a democratic culture.

I will go so far as to suggest that there is no democratic culture without public education—for both our present and our future. As far back as the 1830s, free public education has been promoted as a "crucible of democracy, a blending of all children to function from a common set of values."[6] If we don't understand how to make our public schools more centers of democratic culture, our way of life as a self-governing people is at risk.

3

PASSION VERSUS PURPOSE

—⟋⟍—

Rudy Crew

I began my teaching career in 1973 in a secondary school in the Pasadena Unified School District, which was deeply mired in the issues of desegregation. After my wife and son, my students were the greatest source of joy, inspiration, and passion. I woke up optimistic, went to work energized, and left gleefully exhausted. Every day was an occasion for hope. I thought that was all it took to enable change—that somehow there was a symbiotic relationship between my optimism and the performance of my students, as there was between the broken windows of my classroom and the resistance of parents to meet me during open house. I truly believed that if I simply cared more and demonstrated this as a teacher, it would make up for the gerunds and participles about which my students had no knowledge or would cover the gaps between their current lives and their future aspirations. In short, I was sure that optimism, passion, and a sense of paying forward were sufficient. I soon learned otherwise.

The office of Superintendent Ramon Cortines was directly above my classroom, and it was not uncommon for Dr. Cortines to visit classes unannounced. One day, when I was teaching a lesson on writing style, he and two other official-looking people came into my classroom and observed for what seemed like a very long time. After twenty minutes or so, Dr. Cortines asked the students if they understood the *purpose* of the lesson. Each answer was staggeringly different. The bell rang, dismissing the class, and I was saved—or so I thought.

Dr. Cortines stayed longer and asked me directly, "Did you have a purpose for the last fifty minutes of instruction time?" Then, "Did you have a purpose in mind for the semester? The year?" I answered in the affirmative but realized that I could only muster words of passion, belief, commitment. As a disciple of Ron Edmonds, I knew that language by heart. But the fact that my superintendent sat down and asked that I join him for a longer conversation suggested that he wanted much more. He wanted a ground-zero execution plan for these children. He wanted to know how I was going to plan for those who didn't know, didn't have, and seemingly didn't care. He pushed me hard, and I landed even harder.

I went home less joyous that night. I was a first-year teacher whose passion and love of children had fallen short of being enough. I learned that purpose, planning, strategy, and skill were the next chapters in my growth—that without them I was a surgeon using hope as my only tool.

Fast-forward to my administrative career as a secondary principal and, ultimately, as chancellor of New York City Schools. I was now the one visiting classrooms and having conversations with principals and teachers after minutes or hours spent in their classrooms and their schools. What I knew then and now was that I would always find passion and dedication in teachers and school leaders. Like I once had, they were using the language of their heart. But now, like Ramon Cortines, I needed more.

The war against lost confidence and academic failure seemed not to be won by simply valuing and loving children but by possessing the technical knowledge and skill to teach them. These teachers and school leaders needed strategies that would work in a hugely diverse classroom of learners. Like me, they brought desire. But the teachers in the New York City schools, and especially in the Chancellor's District, brought something more: knowledge of their content, specific strategies, and a willingness to extend their repertoire. This was a whole new language to me. It far surpassed my sense of fear and replaced it with questions about language acquisition, brain theory, and adult learning. I learned how developing teachers' hope and optimism must work in unison with their skill in order for students to succeed. I also listened for that blended voice—that harmony—when hiring principals and school leaders in general.

I was a first-year teacher whose passion and love of children had fallen short of being enough.

After spending four years studying management theory at Babson College, I well understood that capitalism was a system predicated on optimism. It assumed that people would operate out of their base instincts and in so doing strengthen the flow of currency in the marketplace. The essential element of leadership, I thought, was the creation of the optimal conditions under which market choices were readily available, easily understood, and cost effective. So in working in the environment of urban schools, I was naturally curious about how the market system that seemingly does so well in the larger economy can tap into the deep, human desire of people—like those in my neighborhood—to strive for a better life through education. More important, as I became a teacher, the concept that parents—as consumers—and teachers in schools could be led seemed obvious, but in reality less so. Leadership seemed more studied. I thought it was a series of maxims and principles that were to be followed much like a recipe: there would (somehow) be a good outcome by being ultra-precise in its execution. And, perhaps most important in my marketplace notion of education, I thought high profit margins would go to those leaders whose entrepreneurship and innovation were fulfilled with the desire of parents, teachers, and community.

Several secondary school principalships later, however, I could see, and resent, how the schooling culture by and large offered no space for reward, innovation, or entrepreneurship. The school level was designed to promote sameness and *stillness* of ideas, design, and architecture. It was an enormous struggle to accept that intellectual sameness would win over creativity and the artistry of crafting new structures in which children, parents, and teachers would find joy and enthusiasm in learning. I realized that remaining in a leadership role in urban schools would always mean living the tension between the organization's natural inclination to control and my own natural inclination for artistry and movement.

The Chancellor's District in New York City and the School Improvement Zone in the Miami–Dade County Public Schools came out of a desire to redesign and allow teachers to be partners, think outside of the box, and bring about change in the classroom that influenced the district as a whole. The School Improvement Zone encompassed thirty-nine schools marked historically by poor performance, and the Zone students represented groups that had been truly disenfranchised. The focus placed on these children not only improved their lives, but changed everyone's belief in the system. Change is about relationships—adults and children, specifically teachers and students—and these innovative schools' culture of change moved everybody involved into a new "zone" where they were thinking about, acting on, and making assumptions about what it takes to educate all children.

> *Change is about relationships—adults and children, teachers and students—and these innovative schools' culture of change moved everybody involved into a new "zone."*

Unfortunately, the secondary school culture in these districts "drank the Kool-Aid" by believing the maintenance of the existing structure was adequate and has yet to recover. Watching the growth of small schools in New York was the cause for optimism that the central structure (even as I ran it) was still too brittle to fully appreciate the potential for change.

The Parent Academy in Miami-Dade seemed an appropriate and useful way to create a new product. It was based on a well-developed thesis and built on a strong foundation. After all, parents are at the heart of student learning and at the center of any strategic conversation. The Parent Academy offered more than a hundred classes in convenient locations across the district and created the means by which parents and others could enter the parent-student-teacher dialogue as empowered, knowledgeable participants. The response to this new product was overwhelming—in terms of both the community's support for the effort, which was funded entirely by donations, and the more than 100,000 parents who were served. Its success is well known, and the model is being replicated throughout the nation.

The biggest challenge facing today's education leaders, however, is the focus on test scores that comes at the expense of other content and extracurricular activities. I understand the value of an assessment that measures how our students are achieving against state standards and of accountability for results in promoting improvement, but school reform efforts must not overlook the value of, say, physical education in a nation beset by childhood obesity or of arts education in a global economy driven by creativity and innovation. Test results tell us only where students have been, not how far they will go. Passing a test cannot be the driver of expectations. Academically, we need to worry less about how students score on a test and instead look at their ability to write, to analyze, and to understand different cultures. Students will live, work, and compete in a global economy, and so our goal should be a simple one: to ensure that our schools deliver an education that prepares students to graduate ready for college and the careers the global economy offers.

We have all the pedagogy we need, but without a strategy and essential skills, we miss the mark. And, as a consequence, parents in poor communities do not have the same opportunities to benefit from the marketplace of ideas, innovation, and new practice.

4

WHAT SCHOOLS CAN DO IN A DEMOCRATIC SOCIETY

—᙮᙮᙮—

Larry Cuban

I used to think that public schools were vehicles for reforming society. And now I think that while good teachers and schools can promote positive intellectual, behavioral, and social change in individual children and youth, schools are (and have been) ineffectual in altering social inequalities.

I began teaching high school in 1955 filled with a passion to teach history to youth and help them find their niche in the world while working toward making a better society. At that time, I believed wholeheartedly in words taken from John Dewey's *Pedagogic Creed* (1897): "education is the fundamental method of social progress and reform."

And I tried to practice those utopian words in my teaching in Cleveland through the early 1960s. While in retrospect I could easily call this faith in the power of teaching and schooling to make a better life and society naive or unrealistic, I refuse to do so because that passionate idealism, that innocence about the complex and conflicted roles that schooling plays in a

25

democratic, market-driven society gave meaning and drive to the long days working as a teacher, getting married, starting a family, and taking university classes at night toward a master's degree in history.

That confident belief in the power of schools to reform society took me to Washington, D.C., in 1963 (arriving on the day of the civil rights March on Washington) to teach returned Peace Corps volunteers how to become teachers at Cardozo High School. I stayed nearly a decade in D.C., teaching and administering school site and district programs aimed at turning around schools in a largely black city that was a virtual billboard for severe inequalities. I taught history to students in two high schools. I worked in programs that trained energetic young teachers to work in low-performing schools, programs that organized residents in impoverished neighborhoods to improve their community, programs that created alternative schools and districtwide professional development programs for teachers and administrators. While well-intentioned federal and D.C. policy makers attacked the accumulated neglect that had piled up in schools over decades, they adopted these reform-driven programs haphazardly without much grasp of how to implement them in schools and classrooms.

I have few regrets for what I and many other like-minded individuals did during the 1960s. I take pride in the many teachers and students who participated in these reforms who were rescued from deadly, mismanaged schools and ill-taught classrooms. But the fact remains that by the early 1970s, with a few notable exceptions, most of these urban school reforms I and others had worked on had become no more than graffiti written in snow. And the social inequalities that we had hoped to reduce persisted.

Since the early 1970s, a succession of superintendents and elected school boards have descended on the D.C. public schools determined to fundamentally change that benighted district. Even after reforms aimed at the governance, curriculum, instruction, and organization of schools were adopted, even after the glories of parental choice, charter schools, and market competition have been championed as cure-alls for urban district ills—after decades of unrelenting geysers of reforms, schooling in D.C. (now under mayoral control) and most other urban districts remains an educational disaster zone and a blight on a democratic society.

After leaving D.C., my work as a superintendent, professor, and researcher into the history of school reform and teaching led me to see that the relationship among public schools, reform, and society was far more entangled than I had thought. I came to understand that the United States has a three-tiered system of schooling based on performance and socioeconomic status.

Top-tier schools—about 10 percent of all U.S. schools—such as selective urban high schools in New York, Boston, and San Francisco and schools in mostly affluent white suburbs such as New Trier High School (Illinois), San Ramon Valley (California), Montgomery County (Maryland), meet or exceed national and state curriculum standards. They head lists of high-scoring districts in their respective states. These schools send nearly all of their graduates to four-year colleges and universities.

Second-tier schools—about 50 percent of all schools—frequently located in inner-ring suburbs (e.g., T. C. Williams High School in Alexandria, Virginia), often meet state standards and send most of their graduating classes to college. But, on occasion, they slip in and out of compliance with federal and state accountability rules, get reprimanded, and continue on their way as second-tier schools.

Then there is the third tier of schools located in big cities, such as D.C., Philadelphia, Detroit, New Orleans, St. Louis, Atlanta, and rural areas where large numbers of poor and minority families live. Most schools in these cities are low-performing and frequently on the brink of being shut down because they are on federal and state lists of failing schools. Occasionally, a stellar principal and staff will lift a school into the second tier, but staying there is uncommon.

In such a three-tier systems, schools cannot remedy national economic, social, and political problems or dissolve persistent inequities. Schools in these tiers cannot be the vanguard for social reform—ever. Public schools, I have concluded, are (and have been) institutions for maintaining social stability (and inequalities), yet—and this is a significant *yet*—good teachers and schools can promote positive intellectual, behavioral, and social change in many children and youth even in the lowest tier of schools.

The irony, of course, is that many current policy makers, from President Obama through local school board presidents and superintendents, still mime John Dewey's words and act as if schools can, indeed, reform society. In President Obama's 2010 State of the Union speech, for example, he said, "In the twenty-first century, the best antipoverty program around is a world-class education."[1]

So nearly a half-century of experience in schools and the sustained research I have done have made me allergic to utopian rhetoric. Both my experience and research have changed my mind about the role of schools in society. I have become skeptical of anyone spouting words about schools being in the vanguard of social reform—even from a president I admire. Yet, I must confess that in my heart, I still believe that content-smart and classroom-smart teachers who know their students well can make significant differences in their students' lives even if they cannot cure societal ills.

—w—

I used to think that structural reforms would lead to better classroom instruction. And now I think that, at best, such structural reforms may be necessary first steps toward improving instruction but are (and have been) seldom sufficient to alter traditional teaching practices.

In teaching nearly fifteen years, I had concluded that policies creating

Nearly a half-century of experience in schools and the sustained research I have done have made me allergic to utopian rhetoric.

new structures (e.g., nongraded schools, new district and school site governance structures, novel technologies, and small high schools with block schedules, advisories, and student learning communities) would alter common teaching practices, which, in turn, would get students to learn more, faster, and better.

I revised that conclusion, albeit in slow motion, as I looked around at how my fellow teachers taught and began to examine my own classroom practices. I reconsidered the supposed power of structures in changing teaching practices after I left the classroom and began years of researching how teachers have taught following the rainfall of progressive reforms on the nation's classrooms in the early twentieth century and similar showers of standards-based, accountability-driven reforms in the early twenty-first century.[2]

Still, the job of policy makers is to traffic in structures. The belief that these structural changes will alter traditional classroom practices is in the DNA of policy makers. Moreover, class-size changes, national core standards, small high schools, deploying 1:1 laptops, and other structural changes are visible to both patrons and participants. Such visibility suggests vigorous action in solving problems and has potential payoff in votes and longer tenure in office.

As I write, this generation of policy makers invokes that faith in visible structures. They tout changing urban districts' governance from elected school boards to mayors running the schools. Federal and state policy makers champion new structures to evaluate and pay teachers for their success in raising students' test scores. And, of course, they beat the drums loudly for new structures expanding the supply of schools from which parents can choose, such as charters, magnets, and other publicly funded alternatives. Entrepreneurial policy makers assume that these new structures will lead to teachers altering their classroom behaviors and, thereby, improved student learning.

Yet my research and that of others deny the genetic links between structures and teaching practice. Like others, I have concluded that working directly on individual and collective teacher norms, knowledge, and skills at the school and classroom levels—not big-ticket structural changes—have a far better chance of improving teaching practices. Getting policy makers to shift their emphasis from creating new structures to attending to school and classroom routines, however, will be most difficult, since evidence from studies that contradict conventional policy-maker wisdom has a long history of being ignored.

—⁂—

I used to think that the teacher was critical to student and school success. And now I continue to think the same way. I have not changed my mind about the centrality of the teacher to student learning and school performance. The years I spent in classrooms as a teacher, the years I visited classrooms as a superintendent, and the years I studied classroom teaching have strengthened my belief in the powers teachers have in influencing their students' minds and hearts. The tempered optimism I have to-

I have not changed my mind about the centrality of the teacher to student learning and school performance.

day about schooling children and youth rests in this belief in teachers who have made and continue to make a difference in individual students' lives.

That a scrum of research studies and policy-maker pronouncements in the past few years has affirmed teachers' influence in students' academic performance and actual lives supports the faith that I and many other educators have had in teachers. Facts and faith merge nicely.

Yet the current anti–teacher union rhetoric so popular among the entrepreneurial class and the continuing condescension of so many policy makers toward career teachers who have remained in classrooms erode both faith and facts; they eat away at any gains in respect teachers accrued in the past decade.

These three *I used to think . . . and now I think* reflections extracted from nearly a half-century of experience- and research-produced knowledge get at the heart of public schooling in America, especially in cities. That many (but by no means most) schools with skilled and knowledgeable teachers can promote civic, scientific, math, and other forms of literacy, preparation for college, independent decision making, and thoughtful deliberation in children and youth is central to what schools can do in a democratic society even in the lopsided, three-tiered system of schooling that perpetuates long-standing societal inequities.

5

POLICY IS THE PROBLEM, AND OTHER HARD-WON INSIGHTS

—ᴖᴖ—

Richard F. Elmore

At the end of a course or a professional development session, I frequently ask the learners I work with to reflect on how their thinking has changed as a consequence of our work together. This reflection takes the form of a simple two-column exercise. In one column, I ask them to complete the phrase, *I used to think . . .* , and in the other, *And now I think . . .* People often find this a useful way to summarize how our work together has changed their thinking and their habits of mind, and how we have influenced each other.

Recently, at a seminar on the future of school reform, I asked my colleagues—a group of people who have long been active in various strands of school reform—whether they would be interested in doing this exercise as part of our work together. My suggestion was greeted with nearly universal rejection. The possibility

33

that one's work might have changed one's mind over a long period of time seemed just a bit over the edge for that group.

So I decided that I would take the occasion of the twenty-fifth anniversary of the *Harvard Education Letter* to try this exercise myself. I have been working in and around the broad area of school reform for nearly forty years. This period has been the most active time of flux in the history of education in this country. How has my thinking changed?

—⁂—

I used to think that policy was the solution. And now I think that policy is the problem. I am a child of the 1960s—the New Frontier, the Great Society, the civil rights struggles, and the reframing of the role of the federal government in the education sector. I began my career working as a legislative affairs specialist at the cabinet level in a federal agency. I am the product of a public policy program. I taught for eleven years at a public policy school. And I have chaired the Consortium of Policy Research in Education, an association of universities engaged in research on state and local education policy.

Now I have to work hard not to show my active discomfort when graduate students come to me and say, as they often do, "I have worked in schools for a few years, and now I am ready to start to shape policy." Every fiber of my being wants to say, "Use your time in graduate school to become a better practitioner and get back into schools as quickly as possible. You will have a much more profound effect on the education sector working in schools than you will ever have as a policy actor."

What caused this shift? Every day, as I work with teachers and administrators in schools, I see the effects of a policy system that has run amok. There is no political discipline among

34

elected officials and their advisers. To policy makers, every idea about what schools should be doing is as credible as every other idea, and any new idea that can command a political constituency can be used as an excuse for telling schools to do something. Elected officials—legislators, governors, mayors, school board members—generate electoral credit by initiating new ideas, not by making the kind of steady investments in people that are required to make the educator sector more effective. The result is an education sector that is overwhelmed with policy, conditioned to respond to the immediate demands of whoever controls the political agenda, and not invested in the long-term health of the sector and the people who work in it.

This condition seems to be a result of our particularly American form of political pluralism. It is not—I repeat *not*—the case in the other industrialized democracies in which I work, Canada and Australia. My own diagnosis is that this condition is a consequence of an extremely weak professional culture in American schools. Policy makers do not have to respect the expertise of educators, because there are no political consequences attached to that lack of respect.

For the future, I am putting my energy into building a stronger profession, not into trying to repair a desperately dysfunctional political system. For example, I am trying to build a practice that educators can use to observe instruction, in order to develop and strengthen the professional culture of schools. My work is increasingly focused on direct engagement with practitioners, rather than trying to "fix" schools with policy.

—␣∿␣—

I used to think that people's beliefs determined their practices. And now I think that people's practices determine their beliefs.

As a child of the 1960s, I believed in the power of ideas to shape people's behavior. I believed, for example, as many in my generation did, that the problems of failing schools originated in the failure of educators to "believe" that all children were capable of learning or—to choose a more contemporary framing of the issue—that changing teachers' attitudes about what children can learn would result in changing their practices in ways that would increase student learning.

The accumulated evidence, I regret to say, does not support this view. People's espoused beliefs—about race and about how children learn, for example—are not very influential in determining how most people actually behave. The largest determinant of how people practice is how they have practiced in the past, and people demonstrate an amazingly resilient capacity to re-label their existing practices with whatever ideas are currently in vogue.

As practitioners, we are notoriously poor observers of our own practice and therefore not very good at judging the correspondence between our beliefs and our behavior. I know this about my own practice—as a teacher and as a consultant— which is why I rarely, if ever, practice solo any more.

Resilient, powerful new beliefs—the kinds of beliefs that transform the way we think about how children are treated in schools, for example—are shaped by people engaging in behaviors or practices that are deeply unfamiliar to them and that test the outer limits of their knowledge, their confidence in themselves as practitioners, and their competencies. For example, presenting students with learning challenges that adults think are "too hard" for their students often reveals to the adults that the problem lies less in children's abilities than it does in their own command of content and pedagogy. In many instances, our greatest successes in school improvement stem from scaffolding the adults' content knowledge and pedagogy up to the level of what we know students can handle. In these cases, adult beliefs about what children can learn are changed by watching students do things that the adults didn't believe that they—the students—could do.

You don't really know what your espoused beliefs mean until you experience them in practice. The more powerful the beliefs, the more difficult and seemingly unfamiliar the practices. I now care much less about what people say they believe and much more about what I observe them to be doing and their willingness to engage in practices that are deeply unfamiliar to them.

> *I now care much less about what people say they believe and much more about what I observe them to be doing and their willingness to engage in practices that are deeply unfamiliar to them.*

I used to think that public institutions embodied the collective values of society. And now I think that they embody the interests of the people who work in them. I blanch visibly when I hear educators say, "We're in it for the kids." This phrase is a monument to self-deception, and, if I could, I would eradicate it from the professional discourse of educators. Public schools, and the institutions that surround them, surely rank among the most self-interested institutions in American society. Local boards function as platforms and training beds for aspiring politicians. Superintendents jockey for their next job while they're barely ensconced in their current one. Unions defend personnel practices that work in a calculated and intentional way against the interests of children in classrooms. School administrators and teachers engage in practices that deliberately exclude students from access to learning in order to make their work more manageable and make their schools look good. All of these behaviors are engaged in by people who routinely say, "We're in it for the kids." The explanation for these behaviors is not that the individuals are unusually immoral, corrupt, or venal; the explanation is that they are people acting according to their interests.

For twenty years, in my class on politics and public policy, I have tried to convince my students that the first step in acting consistently with what they believe to be "the public interest" is to disabuse themselves of the view that they, and the institutions they inhabit, somehow automatically represent interests broader than their own. In short, you have to know your own interests before you can pretend to represent someone else's interests, and then you have to respect the fact that their interests are *not* yours. To say that the adults in public institutions "represent" the interests of their clients—children and families—is self-deceptive and irresponsible. To say that you are aware of your own interests, and that you are respectful enough of the divergent interests of your clients to listen to them and respond to them as actual people, rather than as constructs of your own view of what's good for them, is to deal honestly and responsibly with your own role. The great leaders of social transformation—Gandhi, Martin Luther King Jr., Nelson Mandela—led by providing an opportunity for people to bring their voices and actions to a common endeavor, not by confusing their own interests with those of the people they hoped to help.

These reflections remind me of what William Butler Yeats said about himself as he approached old age. He increasingly saw the world, he said, with "a cold eye and a hot heart." In many ways, I am still the sixteen-year-old who watched the inauguration of John F. Kennedy on a fuzzy black-and-white TV screen in the bitter cold of a bleak small town in central Washington State and saw a powerful new direction for my life. In other ways, I see the work with a colder eye.

6

FROM PROGRESSIVE EDUCATION TO EDUCATIONAL PLURALISM

—⚶—

Howard Gardner

Almost everyone has a philosophy of education, explicit or implicit, conscious or not. The sources of these personal philosophies are various. Sometimes, the philosophy comes out of one's personal experience ("I loved the Montessori School and everyone should have that education" or "I hated the Waldorf School and please spare the rest of humanity from that experience"). Sometimes the philosophy emerges from reading or personal contact ("As soon as I read E. D. Hirsch's *Cultural Literacy: What Every American Needs to Know*, I knew I had found the answer" or "When I visited Summerhill School, my search for the optimal education was rewarded"). Sometimes, these philosophies remain constant. At other times, changes of mind are catalyzed by personal, societal, or historical developments. Most recently, the well-known historian of education Diane Ravitch publicly renounced her previous support of school choice and large-scale standardized testing.

In this essay, I argue that the notion that there is one "best way" to educate everyone—teachers, young people, music students, students with learning disabilities, and so on—is fundamentally misguided. Indeed, the more we learn about the potential of human minds and brains to flourish in response to various cultures, technologies, and historical accidents, the greater the number of viable options grows. By the same token, single modes of assessment are misguided. The lessons I've learned over the decades are: (1) to be ever open to new and powerful ways of educating and (2) to shun those who block the roads of individualized pedagogy as well as those who seek to impose a uniform way of presenting material.

As a student, I was not particularly reflective about educational approaches. My education in Scranton, Pennsylvania, in the 1950s was traditional and unimaginative—lots of workbooks, worksheets, and weekly spelling tests. By contrast, my studies at Harvard in the 1960s were stimulating and pleasurable. Perhaps my most important educational experience at the time was the opportunity to work with psychologist and educator Jerome Bruner, along with literally dozens of highly creative researchers and teachers, on a model social science curriculum for fifth graders called "Man: A Course of Study." This was my first deep exposure to progressive education, and I liked what I read, heard, and observed: the hands-on experiences, the deep exploration of inviting topics, the belief that the questions asked are as important as their answers, and that the reasoning behind questions and answers is crucial. I became a card-carrying enthusiast of progressive education, American style.

Accordingly, my children were educated at progressive schools. As parents, we did not hesitate to criticize those schools, but as a friend remarked insightfully—and perhaps wistfully—at the time, "We would have liked to go there ourselves." After all, there is a great distance between public education in Scranton in the middle of the twentieth century and a progressive education in Cambridge, Massachusetts, in the latter part of that century. Importantly, however, my four children had four entirely different experiences at these schools, and their diverse personal experiences pose important questions about the notion of a single "best education" for everyone, even one that is determinedly progressive.

As one personally committed to progressive education, I was well prepared for my initial visits in the early 1980s to the small northern Italian city of Reggio Emilia, home of what are widely regarded to be the finest preschools on the planet. Initially launched in the post–World War II era, these municipal schools operate on the assumption that children's natural curiosity should be the centerpiece of education. An object (or experience) that captures the children's attention—a shoe, a fax machine, a rainbow, a birdhouse, or a carved lion at the central piazza—can become the focus of curriculum for weeks, even months. As the young students explore this fertile object, they have the opportunity to draw on the "hundred languages" that are the birthright of every child—their senses, available media and symbol systems, the arts, the sciences, the natural world—to gain relevant insights into the various spheres of life in which these objects occupy a role. What is learned and created each day becomes the starting point for the following days' activities. And these learnings are publicly displayed—or "documented"—so that teachers, parents, and other children can share in them and build on them.

Along with other educators, including my mentor Jerome Bruner, I have visited, studied, and learned from the Reggio Emilia approach for thirty years. This flagship educational enterprise has changed my mind about what is possible to achieve with young children, the importance of group—as opposed to individual—learning, and the role that can be played by documentation of learning over days, weeks, and even longer stretches of time. I have also learned how a single educational experiment—conceived fifty years ago by a determined group of citizens—can affect practices all over the world.

Yet shortly after visiting Reggio Emilia for the first time, I undertook a series of trips to China. There I found that my progressive educational philosophy—Italian as well as American style—was sharply challenged. In classrooms in major cities around the country, I saw the same "prefabricated" lessons presented in essentially the same manner. Little latitude was permitted to either teacher or student. Indeed, in one college class in psychology, I was shocked to observe obviously talented students simply repeating the same lesson over and over. When I challenged the teacher about what seemed to be an obvious waste of time, we had an unproductive conversation that she finally terminated with the terse remark, "We've been doing it this way for so long that we know it is right."

Yet, I was also surprised by some of the positive results. In a first-grade art class, I watched the students slavishly copy a model over and over. I wondered whether these six-year-olds could use their developing skills to portray an unfamiliar object—in this case, an Italian stroller that they could not possibly have seen before. Although the teachers protested when I pro-

posed this assignment, I stuck to my guns. To everyone's aston-
ishment, the students were able to draw the stroller with considerable skill—far greater aptitude than would have been shown
by most American youngsters. This experience convinced me
that an effective education can begin with a singular focus on
skill building rather than on the play of unfettered imagination,
and that the skills that are developed, often precociously, have
the potential to be mobilized to more creative ends.

By now, if you know anything about my own scholarly work,
you are probably thinking, "Well, of course this guy is going
to be for pluralization—he's the
'multiple intelligences person,' the
one who argues for different kinds
of minds." I plead guilty to this
charge. At the same time, however,
I can truthfully assert that when I
developed the idea of multiple in-

*In China, I found that my
progressive educational
philosophy—Italian as well
as American style—was
sharply challenged.*

telligences, I was doing so as a psychologist—education was
not on my mind. Many educational applications of multiple intelligences theory, both in the United States and abroad, have
come as a (usually pleasant) surprise to me.

My increasingly firm belief in a plurality of educational approaches arises chiefly through my studies of and adventures
in the realm of educational policy. The training of and pressures on policy makers push them, perhaps ineluctably, toward
a single, simple, universal solution. This inclination emerges
whether the goal is achieving early literacy; teaching algebra;
or determining who is college, graduate school, or police officer material. Even those who preach a plurality of pedagogical
measures often at the same time embrace a single, final measure
of achievement. Sure, you can teach language or mathematics

any way that you like—but in the end we will judge the success of your methods by a single mandated measure, preferably one developed by the Educational Testing Service, that yields a single number and allows you to be compared with every other individual, school, jurisdiction, or nation on this planet.

Progressive educators have always been suspicious of one way of teaching and assessing, and progressively oriented psychologists have challenged the notion of one optimal way of learning. Until recently, however, this position ran up against the cold fact that many classrooms have thirty, forty, or even sixty students per class. Even if one wants to individualize instruction or pluralize the human and technological means for presenting material, there exist neither the time nor the resources to do so. And so, reason those skeptical of pluralism, aspirations for multiple educational pathways can be realized if one is tutoring one-on-one or if one has an extremely favorable teacher-student ratio, but not for the usual conditions that obtain in schools all over the world.

The advent of computing in its various guises promises to change this sentiment for all time. For the first time in history, it is possible to present material, develop skills, and provide feedback that is highly individualized; to deliver material to learners in a multitude of ways; and, perhaps most dramatically, to provide a variety of ways for learners to demonstrate what they have come to understand.

I would be remiss if I did not acknowledge an alternative view of the matter. Among the most successful educational systems in the world are those in East Asia. Following a Confucian model, these systems do indeed lean toward a single mode of presentation and a single mode of assessment. To the extent that these systems produce citizens who are well educated and who can work productively, I would not recommend scuttling them. After viewing firsthand the results of such education in China, no longer would I fall on a sword to promulgate progressive education.

And yet, one has to bear in mind several drawbacks. First of all, not everyone thrives under such a system. Indeed, the personal casualties for those who cannot learn and perform in a lockstep manner can be severe. Second, these apparently uniform approaches are often supplemented, at considerable cost, by personal tutors or afterschool programs. Third, these lockstep systems have depended on a highly homogeneous population with similar values, mores, and highly involved parents. Such homogeneity is fast disappearing on the planet—even in once nondiverse sites like Singapore, Finland, or, for that matter, Reggio Emilia, where now about a quarter of the families are immigrants. Finally, these Confucian sites have a highly professional teaching corps, well paid and widely respected. The East Asian systems nonetheless represent an approach that is effective in their home context and from which, perhaps, valuable lessons can be learned.

Even with respect to my own children, I learned that a system to which I was personally devoted was not equally appropriate for all.

In the face of highly diverse populations, however, any single-minded approach is likely to encounter difficulties. As I recently observed on a trip to Asia, the top-down Confucian approach proves far less successful with classes that include immigrant children from numerous cultures. By the same token, the progressive approach favored in Reggio Emilia often confounds families that expect a more authoritarian approach to teaching and learning.

The challenges confronting educational systems around the globe reflect an important change in educational goals. In the past, much of education the world over was directed toward selection. This mentality strongly affected educational systems around the globe—from the baccalaureate examinations in Western Europe to the thousand-year-old examination systems in Confucian cultures. But if, as is now the case universally, we want to educate the entire population in its glorious diversity, uniform methods are precisely the wrong way to go. Even with respect to my own children, I learned that a system to which I was personally devoted was not equally appropriate for all; surely, we should be at least as ecumenical when we turn our attention to larger educational systems. Progressivism—perhaps not for all; pluralism—three cheers!

This is not an essay in political theory, but I think it appropriate to conclude with two insights, courtesy of the great twentieth-century English thinker Isaiah Berlin. Borrowing an image from the ancient poet Archilochus, Berlin distinguished between the hedgehog, who knows one big thing, and the fox, who knows many little things. Whatever hedgehog aspirations I might have, clearly at heart I am a fox. And as such, I incline increasingly to individuation and pluralization rather than to homogenization at all costs.

Berlin also drew an illuminating contrast between negative and positive liberty. While negative liberty simply involves the absence of barriers, positive liberty entails the creation of conditions that allow the agent to act freely. Perhaps the provision of rich technologies and the creation of alternative ways of presenting materials and assessing learning will allow more young people to be educated in the manner that proves optimal for them.

7

FIVE YEARS IS
NOT ENOUGH

—ᴍᴍ—

Beverly L. Hall

I used to think that, with a sense of urgency and a solid re-form agenda, a large urban school district could be well on its way to being transformed in five years. Now I think that it takes five years *just to build the foundation* and that twelve to fifteen years of consistent, multifaceted strategies are required to fully transform an urban school system into an organization that achieves excellence in instruction and educational delivery, in facilities and learning environments, and in business operations. I now know that the complexities of the issues that must be adroitly navigated in order to accomplish these three goals can be challenging at best and overwhelming at worst. Five years is simply not enough time for systemic change.

The challenge is that most urban systems never get to stay the course for even five years, let alone fifteen, primarily because it's so hard to retain consistent leadership. The average urban superintendent's tenure is approximately three years—barely enough time to evaluate the landscape and begin implementing a reform strategy, much less see dramatic results. If I had not focused early on fostering the support of political leaders and the business community, I would have added my name to the list of contributors to that haunting statistic. In fact, but for the intervention of Georgia's then-governor, Roy E. Barnes, who told me that I *could not* leave after only six months on the job, this story would be quite different.

What had me on the verge of leaving had nothing to do with the daunting task of improving student teaching and learning. It was a school board that did not understand its role as policy maker and not day-to-day operator of the school system. So the first order of business was to right that ship, which took the collective will of the community. When I came to Atlanta, I knew that there was a committed and powerful coalition of business and community leaders who were intent on improving the public schools in the city. As the fifth superintendent in ten years, I knew having this coalition of supporters with a firm grasp of the work ahead was crucial in making my tenure stable enough to begin to get the job done.

Even with this community mandate, getting the district's leadership moving in the right direction was difficult. Understanding that the superintendent's authority was compromised by the district's statutory charter—the selection and hiring of the chief financial officer and the general counsel were left to the elected school board, not to the superintendent—the business community put its resources behind getting the charter changed.

It took three full years of legislative work to bring the administration of the Atlanta Public Schools (APS) completely under the superintendent's control and to institutionalize strong ethics requirements limiting the school board's direct involvement with the day-to-day operations of the system.

The revolving door of superintendents, combined with school board micro-management, created an environment in which even teachers doubted the ability of the district to function well and students' ability to learn in the system. In a 1999 survey conducted by the district, nine of ten APS kindergarten teachers admitted that they did not believe that their five-year-old students would go on to graduate from high school. Kindergarten teachers are some of the most optimistic people in the profession. Immediate intervention was required if I had any hope of turning their perception around.

That hope came in the form of implementing research-based comprehensive school reform (CSR) models across the district. I began with Project GRAD (Graduation Really Achieves Dreams), mandated in the lowest-performing schools and implemented with the generous support of corporate and philanthropic partners in the 2000–2001 school year. Project GRAD consists of a strong literacy, math, and student discipline program, with a social services component for students and their families. Over the next four years, other CSR models were rolled out across the district selected from an approved list by each school community. I realized that once these reforms took hold and poor students began to achieve on state-level tests, their progress would be called into question. That's why I volunteered to participate in the National Assessment of Educational Progress (NAEP). NAEP, the nation's report card, would be irrefutable evidence. Since 2002–2003, Atlanta students have posted the greatest gains on NAEP compared to other participating urban districts.

Implementation of these proven reform strategies was not easy. Not only were there more than five hundred teaching vacancies at the start of the school year in 2000, but also many of the veteran employees—inside the classroom and out—were unprepared or unwilling to implement the reforms with fidelity. Some were jaded by the revolving door of superintendents and reform fads. Some were angry about the idea of being accountable for doing even more in what they viewed as impossibly challenging environments. As we improved our recruitment and hiring practices to aggressively recruit and get top candidates "on the bus," we also saw waves of retirements and employees electing to get *off* the bus to work in other metro-area districts. Two of every three principals were replaced in the first five years of our program of reform.

Realizing that there was no ready-made pool of qualified leaders capable of executing our new strategy, we developed our own in-house leadership development programs to groom the best and brightest for future leadership positions in the district. Now many of our principals and other leaders come from this program.

Another unexpected challenge was building a senior team of professionals. It was nearly impossible to convince the best people—particularly on the business side of the house—to come to work for a district known for dysfunction and unstable leadership. It took me four or five years to build a competent senior team, and I had to replace some positions three or four times in the first five years.

On arrival in Atlanta, I was pleased to discover that Atlanta taxpayers supported the system in a local referendum to add a one-penny local sales tax to help renovate and construct schools. Citizens have extended that sales tax twice, resulting in almost all of the schools being either new or having significant renovations.

In contrast to the construction program were the district's business operations, the woeful state of which I could not have imagined when I arrived. What I quickly discovered was that my five-year plan for system reform would be impossible without improved academic and financial data systems. Therefore, we installed a new financial management system

It took me four or five years to build a competent senior team, and I had to replace some positions three or four times in the first five years.

and a new student information system at the same time—something I would not recommend, but it speaks to the state of affairs at that time.

Our community partners also assisted us by commissioning an audit of district administration and operations. The audit yielded many recommendations for improvements. One of the most important decisions I made was to create an office of strategy and development to ensure that the audit recommendations were implemented. Although we moved with all deliberate speed, it was not until 2009 that the district was able to implement all of the accepted recommendations. Likewise, our finance division did not earn a clean audit until FY2008. That office continues to serve as the catalyst for many process improvements made over the years.

In the first five years, the time that I thought I could transform the district, I was able to obtain a new governing charter to help keep the board in its role; begin implementation of comprehensive school reform designs, particularly in elementary schools; begin getting the right school leadership in place; hire competent senior staff; begin a leadership training program; implement a new student and financial data system; begin implementation of business and operations improvements;

and continue the school construction program. Although these were monumental accomplishments, they were just the required foundation for whole-system reform. I was nowhere near the finish line.

In the second five years, we continued to push our reforms deeper into the organization. I started high school transformation by breaking up large struggling comprehensive high schools into small schools or small learning communities. High school reform presented its own unique challenge. I found that high school teachers were the most resistant to change. I had to hire outside consultants to ensure that the staff implemented the changes with fidelity and didn't fall back into familiar habits. Eleven years into the reform, all of Atlanta's public high schools have been transformed, and we are seeing incredible results in the form of higher attendance, increased graduation rates, and college scholarships.

Once high school was on its way, I turned to middle school by creating two single-gender academies and piloting a new sixth-grade transition program and interdisciplinary instruction in math and science and English/language arts and social studies, first in four middle schools and now in eight of our fifteen middle schools.

Understanding how important it was to get the story out about our process and to sustain and continue to improve on it, community leaders knew that they could not just sit passively by and hope that all would be well. They commissioned a report to provide the city with a clear picture of how far we had come, if we were moving in the right direction, and what the community could do to help. The report found that we were on the right track and set a reasonable expectation for how long it

would take to fully reform the system—twelve to fifteen years. It also
recommended the creation of an
independent body whose mission
would be to help the community
stay engaged in the reform efforts
and to provide financial support

The report set a reasonable expectation for how long it would take to fully reform the system—twelve to fifteen years.

and political will to stay the course even if the superintendent
changed. That entity, the Atlanta Education Fund, was created
in 2007 and continues to be a strong supporter of the district.

Today, I am convinced that it is not the details of the reform agenda so much as the faithful and sustained implementation of that reform agenda that makes the difference. Progress
doesn't necessarily require the same person in the superintendent's chair over time, though that does help. It does require
sustained, stable leadership over time carried out by individuals who are committed to the same vision and who are intent on
building on success rather than reinventing the wheel and personally branding the reform program.

The Atlanta Public Schools are currently navigating un-
charted waters, having reached a place where its goals are in
sight. But it must stay ever vigilant. Six months after a new
board election, the school board, after years of professional development, stability, and coherence, again manifested signs of
political infighting and discord. Once again, the community
stepped up to make sure that all of the successes are not unrav-
eled and the district doesn't fall back into disarray.

The data show that if it can stay the course, it will likely
achieve its goals within the next five years—by the fifteenth year
of the focused reform effort. But I also believe that there will

likely never be a time that it can rest on its laurels. Educating students who come to school from challenging environments will never be an easy endeavor, and improvement must be evolving and constant. It is my hope that the successful model of reform in the Atlanta Public Schools can accelerate this time line for superintendents in Atlanta and across the nation.

8

REFLECTIONS ON
INCLUSION

—⚏—

Thomas Hehir

"The child should attend the school they would attend if they were not disabled." I have spoken those words hundreds of times, as it is a canon of inclusive education.[1] The reasoning behind this is compelling. First, attending the home school—the institution reflecting the population of students that naturally occurs in the school's population—enables the children to be with their natural supports—brothers, sisters, and friends—and provides them greater opportunities to meet new friends within their community. It reduces the burden on families, as parents do not have to relate to different principals and teachers. For nondisabled students, the presence of students with disabilities from their community demonstrates that disability is a natural part of life and prepares them as well to live in a world in which people with disabilities are integrated into all aspects of life. The principle of having students attend home school has both strong philosophical and managerial justifications.

Philosophically, the doctrine of natural proportions supports the goal of the disability movement: that disability be viewed by the general population as natural and that integration be assumed. Indeed, the Findings section of Individuals with Disabilities Education Act (IDEA) starts with, "Disability is a natural part of the human experience and in no way diminishes the right of individuals to participate in or contribute to society. Improving educational results for children with disabilities is an essential element of our national policy of ensuring equality of opportunity, full participation, independent living, and economic self-sufficiency for individuals with disabilities."[2]

As a former special education director, I supported this principle for administrative as well as philosophical reasons. Serving children in home schools vastly cut down the costs of transportation and resulted in a more even distribution of students throughout the system. This practice also increased the potential for integration into general education classrooms, as no one school or grade had inordinate numbers of students to integrate. And, in study after study, integration into general education classrooms has been associated with improved outcomes for students.[3]

I still support this principle as an ideal. The logic is compelling, and the alternative of segregated, clustered programs organized by disability type reproduces a past that resulted in significant educational inequities. However, after more than two decades of promoting this tenet, I have come to believe that a rigid application of this principle might actually harm some students, particularly those with low-incidence disabilities, those conditions that occur in less than 1 percent of the population, such as blindness, deafness, significant intellectual impairment, etc. I now believe we need a service-delivery system that allows for a variety of options that may or may not be located in the child's home school. The principle of home school placement assumes that eventually all schools will develop the capacity to serve the children who would naturally attend the school. The school would have the specialists on site, and the general education teachers would become skilled in providing accommodations for students with disabilities. In practice, the implementation of home school placement has proved daunting, and other models have developed that may be more desirable for some children.

I have come to believe that the achievement of this ideal is based on several assumptions that have proven formidable in practice and may represent a degree of naïveté concerning school change.

Though I continue to support this principle from both an equity and managerial perspective, I have come to believe that the achievement of this ideal is based on several assumptions that have proven formidable in practice and may represent a degree of naïveté concerning school change.

In order to implement home school policies, schools must develop the capacity to serve a diverse population of students with disabilities in a relatively uniform way; that is, each school must have the capacity to serve a diverse population of students with disabilities. Schools must be able to serve both students with high-incidence or common disabilities as well as those who have more significant or rarely occurring conditions. Approximately 90 percent of students with disabilities fall into five categories of disability: learning disability, mild cognitive disabilities, speech and language disorders, mild to moderate behavioral disability, and other health impairments, such as attention deficit hyperactivity disorder. Taken together, these conditions represent close to 10 percent of children. (See the *Annual Report to Congress on the Implementation of IDEA*.) Given the frequency with which these disabilities occur, and the fact that, in general, the needs of these children are more similar to those of nondisabled students, it is reasonable to expect that most schools develop the capacity to serve these students. Most school districts should, and increasingly do, expect this of their schools.

For students with less common and often complicated needs, the expectation that every school can develop the capacity to serve these students needs to be reconsidered. Though the ideal—that the child attends the same school he would attend if nondisabled—has considerable merit, the ability of each school to meet the needs of students with complicated needs is variable. If No Child Left Behind has taught us anything, it is that many schools struggle even with delivering the standard curriculum. The expectation that a struggling school can then develop the capacity to serve a child with complex needs is clearly questionable.

This is not to say that schools are unable to develop the capacity to serve students with low-incidence disabilities in the school the children would attend if nondisabled. Many schools have. Indeed, many schools in rural areas have been doing this for years because practical alternatives do not exist. In urban areas, there are also effective inclusive schools that have developed the capacity to serve students with very complex needs in the mainstream.[4] However, these schools tend to be exceptionally strong schools overall, with strong leadership and highly skilled teachers. Although they may represent the ideal situation, the expectation that highly effective schools can be replicated on the broad scale has yet to be shown.[5]

Given the unrealistic expectation that all schools will develop the capacity to serve students with complex needs, the second assumption that needs to be questioned is whether clustering students with a particular disability is always undesirable. In addition to the problem of whether the goal of high-quality education for students with disabilities is achievable in all home schools, there is the question of whether this arrangement is desirable for every student with complex or low-incidence needs both educationally and socially.

The proposition that all children be served in their home schools means, mathematically, that most children with low-incidence disabilities will likely be the only child in their age group with their type of disability. While this may represent an integrative ideal, the need for students with disabilities to have associations and friendships with others with similar disabilities has long been recognized by writers with disabilities. Judy Heumann, one of the leaders in the disabilities rights movement and a strong advocate for inclusion, speaks fondly of her experience attending a summer camp for children with physical disabilities.[6] Adrienne Asch, a blind woman who was fully included in her home school in New Jersey in the 1950s, has written about the importance of meeting other blind people for her development.

Heumann and Asch argue for the importance of children meeting other children with similar disabilities as an important part of identity formation and political solidarity.

Neither Heumann's nor Asch's insights are in and of themselves arguments against home school placement. Both of these advocates have strongly supported this principle. However, their writing does argue for the importance of children meeting other children with similar disabilities as an important part of identity formation and political solidarity. If a child is the only student in the school with a particular disability, it is important to create opportunities for her. This can happen naturally if she attends a school with others who have similar disabilities.

Educationally, the needs of these students are diverse and complex. One of the debates that has swirled around special education for decades is whether special education is specialized.[7] As we have responded to the demands to provide appropriate education to all children with disabilities, we have developed highly specialized approaches that should lay this debate to rest. We have developed techniques to provide previously nonverbal students the ability to speak through computer-assisted devices. We have developed behavioral approaches that enable children with autism to engage in instruction within integrated settings. Skilled educators can assist deaf children whose primary language is American Sign Language to learn to write at high levels in Standard English. These are but a few of the specialized interventions and supports that have been developed over the past thirty years, and they represent major advances that can greatly enhance educational access for thousands of children.

Some might argue that the regular education teaching force should be trained to implement these techniques. This makes sense for the disabilities that teachers see frequently, such as dyslexia. Every teacher needs to understand how to address the needs of these students in their classrooms through accommodations and universally applicable teaching methods. However, this logic falls apart when it comes to students with infrequently occurring disabilities whose needs are complex. It makes no sense to train all teachers in educating deaf children when a teacher may not have a deaf child in her class for years at a time.

Given these real problems with the implementation of the home school principle, I believe we must actively support the development of more schools that specialize in the education of students with low-incidence needs, particularly in areas where the population is sufficient to support such schools. Examples of such schools already exist. One is the Henderson School in Boston, which began as an inclusive education initiative in 1989, led by a dynamic principal, Bill Henderson, who is also blind. (At the time, the school was named the O'Hearn; it was renamed in Bill's honor on the occasion of his retirement.) When Bill began his reforms, he designed the school with the assumption that 20 percent of the students would have significant disabilities, mostly students with intellectual disabilities. The model developed at the school, which included two teachers in each classroom, was supported by the budget, which was generated by the presence of a large number of students with significant disabilities, who tend to require considerable resources regardless of setting. Over the years, this school has developed significant organizational capacity in educating students with complex needs. Both special and general educators have had to constantly innovate to meet the needs of these students and have a deep understanding of how to educate these children in inclusive environments.[8]

Another school in Boston, the Mary Lyons, was designed to provide inclusive education for students with significant emotional disturbances. This population has proven particularly difficult for educators to serve effectively, and they experience the poorest outcomes of all disability groups.[9] Yet, at the Lyons, these students are achieving at high levels while at the same time being educated in mainstream environments.[10]

The important dimension that separates the Henderson and the Lyons from home schools is the concentration of a significant number of students with the similar disabilities in a mainstream school. Further, the leaders of these schools were given the resources generated by the students to develop capacity within the general education program. Typically, a single child does not represent enough resources to do this. What distinguishes these schools from typical segregated cluster programs still prevalent in many cities, including Boston, is the fact that these schools have been designed to meet the needs of students with complex needs within inclusive environments. These schools are fundamentally different from traditional urban schools in design, classroom practice, and culture.[11] The presence of a large group of students with significant disabilities coupled with the desire to be inclusive has fundamentally changed these schools for the better for all students. These schools are high performing for *all* students, having some of the highest test scores in Boston. It appears that designing schools to meet the needs of students with the most complex needs are benefiting all students.

So, now I do not simply say, "the child should attend the school he would attend if he were nondisabled." I have shifted my view to allow for more diversity in service-delivery systems. I am more apt to say that children with disabilities should have access to both home school options as well as highly specialized inclusive settings designed to meet the needs of students with complex, low-incidence needs. This more nuanced view may not lend itself to a neat sound bite, but it is born out of experience, research, and the interests of children.

9

IDEAS HAVE SHARPER EDGES
THAN REAL PHENOMENA

—⚅—

Jeffrey R. Henig

I was drawn into researching and writing about education by an interest in big clashing theories and ideologies, not by any intrinsic fascination with what goes on inside schools and classrooms. I was trained as a political scientist, not an educator, and for me the key battles seemed to be about public versus private, government-led versus market-based reforms. I was writing about the politics of privatization for several years before I began to focus in particular on these battles as played out around vouchers, charter schools, and the politics of school choice.

The law of the instrument holds that if you give a child a hammer, every problem will look like a nail. I came out of graduate school equipped to decipher broad political conflicts and to sniff out raw group and class conflict lurking behind claims about knowledge and expertise. When educators talked about curriculum, pedagogy, and cognitive development, my disciplinary preparation led me to suspect that this was their clever way of claiming the privilege to do things to suit themselves and beat back efforts to make them responsive to parents, elected officials, and democratic oversight and control.

I still value and constantly draw on the conceptual tools provided by political science, but I've learned over time that ideas have sharper edges than real phenomena, that knowing something about how things really operate is as important as recognizing that claims about knowledge can be bogus and self-serving, and that not all the important levers of progressive change are the ones that interest groups battle over and policy makers have in their hands.

—∞—

I used to think that markets and government represented distinct arenas, and that education policy was about choosing between them. And now I think that markets and government are intricately and inescapably intertwined. Government has no choice but to enlist the private sector as an ally. This goes beyond the obvious point that government needs tax revenues if it is to do anything at all. Even when they are funded by government, steered by government, and staffed by public employees, schools and school systems need products and services generated by private publishers, testing companies, and building contractors. Even in strong union districts, private labor markets have much to do with the long-term supply and quality of teacher applicants.

Markets are equally dependent on government, not just in the obvious sense that they need laws, courts, and police to provide the safe and orderly environment on which contracts and exchange depend. Outside of small and informal bartering arrangements, markets are politically constructed affairs in which government as regulator and major consumer often plays a very critical role in establishing which goods and services will be needed, which providers will have the inside track, and whether demand for key products will be fortified by legal requirements or the augmentation of "natural" demand (e.g., by providing tax credits or vouchers). Textbook publishers and providers of supplemental education services may be private-market actors, but their viability depends more on how well they sell themselves and their favored policies to government than on marketing their products door-to-door.

In education, recognizing the complex interdependencies between public and private can help defuse otherwise pitched battles. States, cities, and school districts should be able to engage in pragmatic privatization—carefully considered efforts to build, shape, and use markets in support of democratically mediated goals—without fear that this necessarily constitutes a first step on the slippery slope of systemic privatization, in which the core institutions, values, and capacity of the public sector are irreversibly undermined. Pragmatic privatization can give public officials tools to increase flexibility,

In education, recognizing the complex interdependencies between public and private can help defuse otherwise pitched battles.

variety, and innovation and extend their reach into areas in which the existing bureaucracy lacks capacity and expertise. There are risks: for example, if schools become too reliant on particular private providers, they may find themselves dependent and outgunned, unable to call the shots and insist on protecting public values. Recognizing complexity, therefore, does not mean that we should abandon concern that some forms of privatization can spiral out of democratic control, but it should make us less eager to demonize private providers and more interested in finding ways to draw them into the collective project of pursuing the public good.

—⁊⁊—

I used to think that a critical question was, "Are charter schools better than traditional public schools?" Now it is clear to me that the differences among schools within the charter and traditional public school sectors are greater than those between the typical schools within each sector. In the early days of the charter school phenomenon, key organizations on both the Right and the Left decided it was politically savvy to frame the two as distinctly different sectors in a head-to-head battle to determine the future of American education. Conservative proponents of markets discovered that charters were a more consumer-friendly product; they did not spark the sharp resistance met by vouchers, which could be used at private schools. Traditional Democrats saw charters as nothing more than a stalking horse for vouchers and decided that they could still count on Americans' protectiveness toward their public schools to back them up in a battle to kill the charter baby while it was still in the crib.

Missed at the time was the recognition of charters as descendants of a long line of efforts—outside and inside education—to decentralize public-sector decision making and loosen the shackles of bureaucratic sameness. Charter schools could have been promoted as part of the reinvention of government—something the Clinton/Gore administration recognized but around which that administration failed to mobilize sufficient support. When I first began to research charter schools back in their early days, I quickly realized that the foot soldiers in that movement were much more like political heirs to the Community Action Agencies of the liberal War on Poverty than intellectual heirs of Milton Friedman.

The research on charter schools is still developing and improving, and it is easy to be distracted by sequential studies that claim one thing ("charter schools are better!") followed on the heels by others claiming the opposite. But two bottom-line observations seem solid and clear. Chartering schools is not a panacea; without strong and effective authorizing and oversight, they can produce schools as mediocre and misguided as the worst traditional public schools. And traditional public schools systems, even massive urban systems like those in Chicago and New York City, are not so hamstrung by bureaucracy and reactionary unions that they cannot initiate substantial change.

Good politics can be wasted if it rides in on the wrong horse, and even good policies falter if they are implemented in a tentative, ill-informed, or unpracticed way.

―※―

I used to think that getting the politics right was more important than figuring out the right thing to do, and that figuring out the right thing to do was more important than figuring out exactly how to do it. Now I think good politics can be wasted if it rides in on the wrong horse and that even good policies falter if they are implemented in a tentative, ill-informed, or unpracticed way. In our pluralist system, it is politics that determines public priorities; groups that lack the muscle or know-how to project and protect their interests will find that their issues and favored policies get short shrift. I used to think that if groups representing the interests of traditionally underserved population mobilized effectively and fought their way into partnership status within local governance regimes, effective policies would fall into line. Sure, sometimes they'd battle for programs that would prove ill conceived, but well-intentioned government should be able to notice and learn from its mistakes; as long as the supporting coalition held together, policy and implementation would progressively improve.

But sustaining political coalitions is extremely difficult in the high-reverberation sound chamber that is American education politics. All allegiances are contingent, because groups are pursuing multiple goals and have little patience for partnerships that fail to deliver the goods. Missteps, even if well-intentioned, echo into a reputation for ineffectiveness. Unless all signs point to progress, innovative superintendents, mayors, governors, legislative champions, and policy entrepreneurs find their support crumbling behind them and then aligning behind a new voice and a new set of ideas. The cycle of ephemeral reform initiatives that run hot, then cold, is repeated again.

It matters, then, whether reform coalitions back the right set of policies and whether they take the time and care to ensure that teachers, schools, and the system have the knowledge and capacity to put them into working order. Coming up with an education agenda that captures enthusiasm is important. So is working out policy designs that are thoughtful and coherent. But these alone only take us so far. Reforms need to do more than gain influence, change the terms of debate, and pass good policies. They need to wrestle with the machinery of government and administration, to put the right people in place, with the right tools and skills, and attend to the sometimes tedious tasks of motivating, coordinating, learning, and adapting so good intentions and good ideas do not go to waste.

10

YOU SAY "EXPERT," I SAY . . . NOT SO MUCH

—⚒—

Frederick M. Hess

I used to think that experts really understood the world. Now I think that they are people who know a great deal about tiny slivers of life, but that this narrow expertise is often of dubious value when it comes to tackling complex challenges or making the world a better place. More to the point, I now think that experts get so taken with their tiny slivers of expertise that they routinely overestimate both how much they know and their ability to produce broad, beneficial change.

Now, don't get me wrong. Most "experts" always struck me as pompous, self-satisfied, pretentious, venal, and biased. But I tended to place some degree of confidence in their particular insight and expertise. And now, as we say, not so much.

While it may not be immediately obvious, all this has had a profound impact on how I think about schooling, education, and policy. Before I go there, however, it might be useful to back up and explain how I got here.

For the longest time, I was taken with the notion of expertise. I can still remember when I was fourteen and my dad promised me that, if I gave my old bike to my younger brother, I could have his beat-up, yellow Honda Civic when I turned sixteen. The catch was that the Civic no longer ran; rather, my dad (a pretty fair bootstrap mechanic) and I were going to fix it.

It sounded like a good deal. That Saturday we headed out to the Honda resting under the carport, and popped the hood to reveal an indecipherable mash-up of hoses, molded steel, and wiring. I can still clearly recall my response to the sight. It pretty much amounted to, *Ah, @#%&!* Tellingly, in that moment, I felt a deep and utter helplessness in the marrow of my bones. One thought, clear and certain, ran through my mind: I could study this engine for a month and it wouldn't make any sense to me. Don't be fooled. There's no happy, touching redemptive story here. I slunk away, threw in the towel, and, when I turned sixteen, bought an old Plymouth Duster for $900.

Now, the engine of a Honda Civic, built in the 1970s, was not, in fact, indecipherable. I had buddies who enjoyed working on cars and found engines to be interesting, manageable puzzles. That experience seemed to illustrate for me how sadly inept I was at things that mattered. For much of my life—through childhood, adolescence, college, teaching, graduate school, and into my tenure as a professor at the University of Virginia—I always labored under the strong suspicion that lots of other people had a perfectly lucid understanding of things that were opaque to me.

I remember as a high school and college student reading about new technology companies, research studies, or arms control negotiations and thinking that the people who were doing these things were incomprehensibly smart and informed.

I'd read book critics and wonder how they could know so much and find such textured nuance in a book I'd found tedious or hear football coaches talk about the enormous complexity of their offensive schemes and be dazzled by their terminology.

I would meet fellow college students full of confidence in their future plans, who seemed to know how the medical or legal profession worked and how to go about getting themselves started. I remember standing in line at the Harvard University campus waiting to take the GRE in political science and listening to all the students chattering about sophisticated political concepts, contacts, and graduate programs. I felt overwhelmed, and tired. How could they know so much?

Along the way, I started to doubt whether I'd ever even be able to find a job. I'd ask myself, "Wow, I know so little and all these successful people know so much; how am I ever going to convince anyone to hire me to do anything?"

Little by little, though, I got the sense that these folks didn't know as much as they claimed. I posted a pretty fair score on that political science GRE, one that suggested I knew as much or more than any in that intimidating cast of characters. When I was admitted to the PhD program in government at Harvard and then won a National Science Foundation fellowship, the chilling possibility occurred to me that I actually *was* a budding expert—in my own little area. That was downright scary, because I knew how little expertise I actually possessed.

Little by little, I got the sense that these folks didn't know as much as they claimed.

I would listen to lectures or read policy proposals and be struck by their seeming naïveté and reliance on wishful thinking. I'd ask an acclaimed guest speaker a question about practical

application or potential unanticipated consequences of their recommendations, and I'd consistently be underwhelmed by their
inclination to rehash their talking points and brush past any
complications. It gradually struck me, as I earned my MEd and
then took my first teaching job, that much of the "expertise" I
encountered seemed to consist of self-promotion, a dubious title,
or misplaced self-confidence.

As I finished my degree, was hired as a professor by a respected university, and started to publish books, articles, and
papers that drew attention from newspapers and leading au-
thorities, it became clear to me that I was indeed now one of
those "experts." I was still utterly confident that I had no business fixing a car, much less the world. And I knew I had no
claim on posing as an unimpeachable source of wisdom. In light
of that, I figured there were only two explanations for my new-
found success. The first, and the one I favored for the longest
time, was that I was a fortunate poseur, a fake, an imposter who
had gotten in over my head and who would be found out in due
time. The second was that I was like a lot of the other experts
and that they actually were (or should be) as hesitant as I to
claim they could fix the world with any precision.

Over time, I've become increasingly convinced that the correct answer was the second explanation. And, let me be clear,
that realization froze my blood. For one thing, I've been surprised at how many successful and respected individuals I
know who, in moments of private candor or over a beer, will
smilingly confess to their own version of the *Am I a fraud?* concern. For another, I've been astonished at the resistance to al-
ternate ways of thinking or seeing that characterizes so many
reputed experts. And I've come to believe that arrogance, traditions of deference, the yearning for verities, and the demands

of hierarchical institutions have as much to do with creating many supposed experts as does actual merit.

In particular, I've been fascinated to see how success in some role (as a CEO, a superintendent, a politician, or what have you) is broadly seen as giving someone entrée to playing the expert in all kinds of venues where they may or may not know what the hell they're talking about.

I gradually became convinced that this phenomenon isn't unique to education or academia. Really, in pretty much any realm where we can measure how expertise fares, its track record is rather weak. Consulting firms have very uneven records of actually improving the state of affairs for their clients. Most professional stock pickers do worse than simple indexes of stocks. Professional talent evaluators have a famously uneven track record in the NFL, NBA, or MLB drafts when predicting the next crop of star athletes. Industry executives have a horrendous record when it comes to predicting which movies, books, or television shows are going to be hits.

And, of course, there are experts like David Lereah, formerly the chief economist for the National Association of Realtors. In 2005, Lereah published a book titled *Are You Missing the Real Estate Boom? Why Home Values and Other Real Estate Investments Will Climb Through the End of the Decade—and How to Profit from Them* and told the *Washington Post* that year that "any talk of the housing market crashing is ludicrous."

Further, we should all keep in mind that I am hardly the first to be struck by the dubious nature of expertise. Aristophanes had great fun with this precise topic more than two thousand years ago, while Jonathan Swift's *Gulliver's Travels* found the academicians of Lagado intent on extracting sunbeams from cucumbers.

Say something smart once and there are huge rewards for spending a career saying it, in increasingly elaborate forms. Academics who own an idea get hired by prestigious universities, deliver keynotes, and get all kinds of attendant perks. Consultants who own an idea become must-haves for districts, foundations, and contractors. The result is a familiar kabuki of hyperspecialists airing their prebaked views.

The world is composed of niches. In each, a thinker may be iconic so long as she stays in her little crevice. Thus, an expert in pharmacology may speak to a cheering conference hall of awe-struck attendees only to walk across the campus or the hotel and quickly become just an anonymous face in the crowd. An expert on school violence or science instruction might be feted as legendary by those in her field but sacrifice that respect and deference should she wander outside that circle. The result discourages individuals from spending much time wrestling with thorny questions or complexities that reach beyond their core expertise. Hence, enormously respected thinkers will offer prescriptions for educational policy or practice that are woefully naive in terms of political dynamics, organizational realities, institutional pressure, incentives, or practical constraints. Why? Because many of these experts have never spent much time thinking about how their expertise intersects with all the stuff in which they're not expert.

Meanwhile, within niches, the interest in weighing competing arguments or determining how one's expertise translates to the larger world is massively undervalued. Expertise promotes deep knowledge, which can too readily lead to inflexibility and self-assuredness (along with the expectation that one's biases and assumptions will be afforded deference). There are always exceptions, but most thinkers become expert by struggling to the top of their niche on the back of their big idea, and then do all they can to extend the reach of that idea and of the acolytes who aid in that quest—incidentally, or quite purposefully, stymieing heterodox perspectives. In fact, the very nature of expertise is that it stifles dissent and reifies the orthodoxy of the moment.

In fact, the very nature of expertise is that it stifles dissent and reifies the orthodoxy of the moment.

Moreover, since established figures typically find themselves addressing friendly audiences and gatherings where it is deemed impolite to contest their assumptions and evidence too ardently, it is frighteningly easy for experts to settle into a comfortable bubble where they are surrounded by like-minded peers and adoring disciples, their word is gospel and they are buffered from anything more than occasional interaction with those who might disagree.

Finally, our criteria for expertise are, almost inevitably, relational (e.g., my colleague tells me Trang is terrific) or formulaic (e.g., Wylie was executive director of X for a number of years, launched Y program, or has published eleven articles on this). Why? Our ability to form independent judgments of the hundreds or thousands of individuals most directly engaged in our field of endeavor, much less the thousands more peripherally engaged, is limited by our own inexpert grasp of the world. Only the arrogant or the deluded imagine they perfectly understand the strengths and skills of hundreds of friends, acquaintances, and strangers. Thus, we turn to proxies that are themselves deeply imperfect—but that can lead to our investing great authority in this or that expert for a season.

Done with sufficient skepticism and care, this manner of finding experts is natural and normal. But there's a decided temptation to lodge excessive influence in our choice of the moment. I can't tell you how many times I've been talking with a superintendent who has become a guru for a foundation and found myself wondering why this unremarkable man was deemed any more deserving of that status than any of a dozen other superintendents. The difference, in many cases, is nothing more than a personal relationship, experience in a few big districts, or the fact that a superintendent was an early adopter of a reform—all of which, perhaps bizarrely, results in an individual being invested with presumed expertise across a broad range of issues.

So why does any of this matter? Does it make any practical difference when it comes to schools or schooling? I think it does. In education, for instance, despite decades of research, experts have no systematic way to tell who will be a good teacher or how to design practices that lead to predictable improvement at scale. This state of affairs means at least four things.

First, we ought to be hesitant in casually suggesting that we can name, based on our experience, a list of the nation's best school districts, superintendents, or reading programs. Short of some protocol that helps us identify excellence in a transparent and consistent fashion (for better or worse), we ought to be much humbler about such exercises. They frequently amount to nothing more than an echo chamber, with participants passing on names that they themselves have received second- or third-hand.

Second, we should be wary of prescriptive advice, especially when it's based on the assumption that expertise easily and immutably travels across contexts. In fact, given its narrowness, expertise can exert a gravitational pull that distorts how one thinks about the larger world. Expertise can come at the cost of perspective when an expert starts contemplating efforts to change policy, organizations, or human behavior. After all, expert advice tends to reflect what experts know, which may not reflect what is most useful for solving the larger problem in the real world. For instance, grand assertions about merit pay, school choice, differentiated instruction, or class-size reduction that overlook the practical impact of contracts, policies, existing incentives, and embedded routines can yield results quite different from those the experts are touting.

Third—all that said—expertise has a terrifically useful place, as long as we understand what the experts actually know, which is how to do specific, concrete tasks right. I'm always eager to turn to an expert when the question is how to build a bridge, estimate how many people will visit Vegas next month, design an assessment, erect a new school, or conduct a complicated statistical analysis. I'm less inclined to do so when the questions are bigger, messier, and more dependent on judgment and values.

Finally, we need to recognize that individual experts ought not be invested with too much prescience, but the right mix of experts can help identify tensions, incentives, and the contours of possible solutions. If one assembles the right mix of experts, their competing views can prove enormously helpful in crafting smart policies. The key, however, is not to empower any one expert to play guru but to allow competing expertise to illuminate and inform complex decisions.

One last thought. For what it's worth, my approach nowadays is not to casually reject educational expertise but to regard its acclaimed ministers with the same attentive skepticism I reserve for financial advisers and real estate agents. They know stuff that's useful, but that doesn't entitle them to blind deference or even trusting obeisance. At least not in my book.

11

HOPE IN THE POSSIBLE

—∿—

Deborah Jewell-Sherman

From the time that I knew myself, I wanted to be a teacher and change the world, because I was early taught that education was life altering. I spent my formative years playing teacher and volunteering in schools, and on receiving my undergraduate degree, I truly thought I knew almost everything about teaching and learning.

However, the ensuing three-plus decades have helped me realize that the more I learn, the more I question; and the longer I have practiced my craft, the less certain I am about many things. Like the characters in the 2009 hit movie *The Blind Side*, I have frequently been upended by the realization that my certitude has been challenged by new evidence. Coupling deep knowledge, commitment, and courage with continuous analysis, questioning, and rethinking has helped me evolve from someone who felt I had all the answers to someone who now welcomes research and experiences that cause me to reevaluate some of my deeply held assumptions, especially about the education of our nation's urban youth. Two areas in which I've significantly shifted my intellectual perspective concern the notion of fixed intelligence and the value of charter schools.

As a child of the fifties and sixties, I took numerous intelligence tests as prerequisites for special placements and to gain entrance into specific schools. Based on these results and other assessments, students of my vintage were labeled within heterogeneous classrooms and within homogeneous tracks as the "smart" students, the "average" ones, and the "struggling" or challenged learners. Just as today, most students of that era understood the ramifications of these labels, regardless of the names assigned to the groupings. And once ensconced in one of the lower-ability strands, it took the equivalent of divine intervention to be moved to a perceived higher-achieving group. Even as a young person, I felt it inordinately unfair that some of my closest friends were not afforded the same opportunities as I was. Clearly, in our limited social world, they seemed able to do all that I could—and in terms of anything athletic far more—so I quietly questioned the perceived inequities of this dual standard. However, my undergraduate studies and student teaching only served to reinforce these perceptions. And it was with this mental mind-set that I began teaching my own students.

I used to think that intelligence was a gift and that it was a matter of luck or an accident of birth as to the amount of the gift you received. As a teacher of youth and adults, I exhorted my students to excel but always within the confines of a fixed ceiling imposed by my understanding of their innate abilities. I recall, with chagrin, how I sat with psychologists, social workers, administrators, and teachers to evaluate students during child study meetings to determine whether they met the criteria for gifted programs or for an individualized educational plan. We spoke in absolute terms about how far individuals would be able to progress academically based on the data collected, with a major focus on each student's intelligence quotient, or IQ.

I now know that no one indicator of ability is a true barometer of what an individual child or group of children is capable of learning

Even as a young person, I felt it inordinately unfair that some of my closest friends were not afforded the same opportunities as I was.

and achieving. While my own teaching and learning strengthened my inner resolve to defy the limits imposed by a child's fixed intelligence, it was the work of two different educators that provided compelling evidence and helped me refute the persistent, limiting perceptions I and others have held about students' innate abilities and intelligence.

In his groundbreaking work *Frames of Mind: The Theory of Multiple Intelligences*, Howard Gardner challenged the notion that one's intelligence could be measured only in terms of verbal and quantitative criteria.[1] Rather, Gardner broadened the concept of intelligence to encompass the multiple intelligences he named linguistic, logical-mathematical, musical, spatial, bodily-kinesthetic, interpersonal, and intrapersonal. Making the connections between his work and mine from a purely clinical perspective would have been daunting; however, his belief that educators had "to convey important ideas and concepts in a number of different formats" and that the "activation of multiple intelligences holds promise of reaching many more students" emboldened me to expand the limits of my thinking about what students needed to know and understand, how teachers needed to think about teaching and reflect on their practice, and what learning was essential for students and what they needed to demonstrate they could do while under my watch.[2]

During my tenure as assistant superintendent for instruction for the Richmond Public Schools, I worked with teachers, principals, and instructional staff to ensure that the teaching and learning of every student was the responsibility of all employees, that the district's model curriculum and best practices were aligned with state and national standards, and that quality teaching was the province and responsibility of all teachers in all disciplines.

In the nineties, Jeff Howard's call for "a new logic in education reform" further enhanced my thinking about the beliefs, policies, and practices educators and administrators needed to embrace if they were to maximize the learning and achievement outcomes for all students.[3] In his work with The Efficacy Institute, Howard stressed that by reforming the policies and revising the practices within classrooms and school districts, all students, and especially those in urban settings, could achieve at high levels and demonstrate success throughout their K–12 continuum and beyond. Specifically, he voiced the belief that this nation's students, including urban youth and children of color, could "master challenging content." Rather than a limited set of expectations, Howard stressed the need for school districts to adopt a "constructivist belief" system that incorporates the use of rigorous curriculum, stellar instructional practices, and transformational professional development, resulting in all learners demonstrating accelerated, measurable improvements in their outcomes.

On assuming the superintendency of the Richmond Public Schools (RPS) in 2002, I knew that no one person turns around a school district. The leadership for the instructional improvement strategies we used in RPS was cultivated from every sector of the district. Together we came to value and know that radical reform and transformation require that educators have a shared mission, vision, and values; that the work needs to be collaborative in its inquiry, experimentation, and accountability; that principal-fostered learning communities within each school are critical for the professional growth and continuous improvement teachers need; and that the work of the organization always needs to be outcome oriented and measured in terms of the significant improvements demonstrated by students' learning and doing.

The true legacy of one's leadership is not measured in terms of the travails one undergoes to enact systemic reform or the plaudits one may receive for having accomplished goals and survived the tumult. Rather, the deep sense of peace and the profound sense of accomplishment I feel as I reflect on my years at the helm of RPS are intrinsically linked to the difference made in the educational outcomes and the opportunities afforded numerous children while their learning was under my watch.

Through the belief and tutelage of many knowledgeable, impassioned, and committed educators, and in concert with parents and partnerships culled from businesses, communities of faith, universities, and other entities, the students in RPS demonstrated exponential improvements in multiple areas during my tenure, and the school district has continued to focus its collective energy on improving teaching and successful learning for all.

—ɷ—

At great personal sacrifice and financial cost, my divorced mother determined that her three children would attend the best schools available. While many of my friends attended our neighborhood public schools, she worked feverishly, often at two jobs, to ensure that we attended Catholic grammar and high schools. My siblings and I received a strong educational foundation, but at a cost. We were expected to adopt the school's way of thinking, behaving, and learning even when it varied from the ethos of our community. Those students who didn't comply were discharged to the public schools.

I honor my mother's commitment and appreciate the learning fostered by my teachers. However, I determined early in my career that no parent should feel compelled to forgo the free public schools because of their inferior educational offerings and that students should not have to forgo their multiple allegiances to family and community to realize academic and career success. Rather, I believed then and now that a stellar public school system, while still a distant reality, is bedrock to the realization of the best tenets of our democracy and that students should be encouraged to function successfully in myriad environments as they maintain their unique characteristics, nurture their innate gifts, and demonstrate that demography is not destiny. As a result, I made improving public schools—classroom by classroom and school by school—my overarching career priority. From its inception, I viewed the advent of the charter school movement as the newest incarnation of my deepest fears about aspects of my own Catholic school education and as a real threat to the realization of my most important systemic goal of improving public schooling.

I used to think that well-educated public school professionals easily could come to consensus about best instructional strategies, would always work in concert with enlightened administrators who promoted innovation, could accept that accountability is the correlate of creativity, and would embrace policies and organizational structures that placed the needs of students, not adults, first. Over the years, I have learned that transforming the education sector, which from my vantage point is nonnegotiable, requires significant changes in the beliefs, mission, design, and daily work by educators and in the policies, governance, and practices of those who lead the enterprise. What I have come to embrace is the educational equivalent of Frederick Douglass's admonition about free-

I believed then and now that a stellar public school system, while still a distant reality, is bedrock to the realization of the best tenets of our democracy.

dom. Douglass avowed that "power concedes nothing without a demand. It never has and it never will." Transforming the education sector will require, among other things, exemplars of best practices to serve as guideposts to excellence, in concert with both incentives for reform and disincentives for the maintenance of the current state of affairs, to encourage and at times force change.

In their article "The Work of Leadership," Ronald Heifetz and Donald Laurie note that "when businesses cannot learn quickly to adapt to new challenges, they are likely to face their own form of extinction."[4] The work currently being undertaken by the likes of Geoffrey Canada in The Harlem Children's Zone's Promise Academy Charter Schools, by Timothy Knowles and Linda Wing in the University of Chicago's Urban Education Institute, and by Steve Perry in the Capital Preparatory Magnet School in Hartford, Connecticut, gives me hope in the possible. Their charters are inclusive of all children while being expansive in their use of instruction and the provision of support for the development of the whole child. They, among others, seek to provide stellar opportunities for the students they serve while modeling strategies that may have utility as public school districts seek large-scale reform.

In unique ways, they evidence that there are charter schools that model entrepreneurial leadership; espouse clear, compelling values, and goals; demonstrate child-centered instructional practices; embrace innovation and creativity; adopt transparent operating practices; and accept accountability measures and continuous improvement as organizational norms.

In spite of my deep-seated reticence, my initial skepticism, and compelling evidence that numerous charters fail miserably, I am now persuaded that charter schools have a valid role to play in the improvement of the public education sector, which is the critical endeavor facing educators today. While maintaining a critical eye and an evaluative stance, educators and leaders in the sector have "a moral imperative" to embrace change and innovation "that comes with the desire to fulfill the hopes of those we serve and those with whom we work."[5] For as I heard PBS commentator Tavis Smiley state in an evening broadcast, "The eyes of the future are looking back on us and hoping that we will do what needs to be done to secure their places."

12

RETHINKING UNIONS' ROLES
IN EDUCATION REFORM

—∿∿—

Brad Jupp

In the spring of 2001, Rich Rosivach and I were on the phone discussing how to position Denver's Pay for Performance Pilot as an acceptable choice to the faculty of Thomas Jefferson High School. It was a critical moment in the pilot, because, although there were thirteen schools on board, not one was a high school. Board members, teachers, and union and community leaders all believed the pilot would prove little unless there were one or two high schools involved. To join the pilot, 67 percent of the faculty had to vote yes on a question to participate.

Rich was TJ's union representative, a star social studies teacher at the beginning of his career and one of the key players in the decision-making drama. Our conversation was about the stuff that school politics is made of: how the science department might vote, whether people would listen to the math department chair, counting the vote of every teacher. Midway through the call, he made a remarkably clearheaded point: "As I see it, we—as teachers, as a union, and as a profession—have two choices. We can fight to maintain a twenty-year-old defensive position holding off reforms like pay for performance. Or we can get out in front of them, lead them, and make them better because we did. I know where I want to be. I don't want to spend the rest of my teaching career, the next twenty-five years, in a continuous rear-guard action. I want to be in front." He was expecting new terms of engagement—leadership, rather than resistance. As I listened, I was persuaded by a resonance grander than other reasons to enter the pilot, one that connected the profession and the union to a constructive and forward-moving direction. In a couple of weeks, after Rich and other union members canvassed the school, TJ's faculty voted to join the pilot.

Rich echoed beliefs I held when I joined the profession in 1986. I was a language arts teacher at Denver's Martin Luther King Jr. Middle School. My head was full of *Death at an Early Age* and *Rules for Radicals*.[1] Jonathan Kozol taught me about the intolerable social injustice that occurs when our most vulnerable children were let down by failing institutions, especially public schools. Saul Alinsky taught me it would take a mass movement, a movement I could see being led by my teacher union, to undo that injustice. When I was talking to Rich, it was easy to see his point. It was almost as easy to believe that the union's members could be convinced that, even in the face of difficult policy decisions, our best posture was our active leadership, not repeated refusal. It was even possible to believe that, if our schools were to thrive, then local, state, and national unions would have to take their place in the advance guard leading the development and implementation of policy, propelling the profession further forward. I believed this in 1986. I believed it in 2001 when I was working with Rich. I still believe it.

But since I believe teacher unions can take a leading role in the improvement of our schools, I must also admit I now believe the work will be much harder than I imagined twenty-five, or even nine, years ago. Yes, there are some exciting, singular examples where union engagement has produced forward-moving results, either in improved student performance or in policy direction. It was Cincinnati and Seattle once and New Haven and Hillsborough County, even Illinois and Delaware, now. But an honest survey of the public school landscape would find their number in the dozens, certainly not the hundreds, few and far between among the nation's fifteen thousand school districts and in its fifty states.

Why so scarce? If I listen to my colleagues in classrooms and union leadership positions, there are plenty of reasons, and they are mainly outside the union hall. For the past twenty-five years, they remind me, the climate of policies and practices in which our schools try to thrive has become harsher. Federal, state, and local reforms, as far back as the Improving America's School Act, came from the top down and were met with the skepticism of teachers, especially when they linked accountability to student performance.

When administrative leaders, often facing sanctions called for by those reforms, accelerated the pace of change, teachers and their unions found the pace random, too fast, or in the wrong direction, and the administration unwilling to listen to their calls to slow down, correct direction, and resist the temptation to choose the reform du jour. At the same time, those calling for reform grew impatient. They drew battle lines with the unions. After repeated clashes, positions didn't move much; they hardened. So when union leaders got out in front and tried to embrace change, as Bob Chase did with "The New Unionism," the effort was too much for many members and not enough for the reformers. History, my colleagues tell me, proves that there is little organizational gain when the local or state affiliate goes out to the leading edge. Creating a culture of engagement is difficult because the external conditions facing unions make it so.

This body of perceptions may be accurate, at least in part. Even if it is not, my colleagues in classrooms and union halls find it powerfully persuasive. Over the course of a career that has enjoyed seats on multiple sides of the policy debate, the bargaining table, and the effort to lead schools forward, I now believe that what makes it so difficult to lead teacher unions forward in reform is as much, if not more so, internal to the unions' own operations.

Bill Slotnik and Lee Bray, colleagues who helped us get the Pay for Performance Pilot off the ground in Denver in 1999, told us, "Your school district is perfectly designed to get the results it is getting right now. If you want different results—whether for students or teachers—you are going to have to change the way the district is designed." Their point is just as relevant to teacher union affiliates as it is to school districts. In their present form, unions are perfectly designed to create a culture of resistance. If we are to see teacher union affiliates take a leading role in improving our schools, we must begin to ask some questions about how they are designed.

I know, having spent so much of my career in union leadership positions, how much I resented it when someone from outside the union rattled off a list of things to do so we would behave differently. My hope is to offer these questions with a different spirit, the spirit of Saul Alinsky, whose words I carried into the job when I first became a teacher. In *Rules for Radicals*, he reminds us that in the face of ever-changing circumstances, the organizer—a character in Alinsky's lexicon who in many ways is an archetype for the union leader—is always skeptical. He accepts the Supreme Court Justice Learned Hand's statement that "the mark of a free man is that ever-gnawing inner uncertainty as to whether or not he is right . . . He must constantly examine life, including his own, to get some idea of what it is all about, and he must challenge and test his own feelings. Irreverence, essential to questioning, is a requisite. Curiosity becomes compulsive."

In my questions, I hope there is less irreverence and more compulsive curiosity. I pose them knowing that, even if I could venture to provide answers myself, what matters now is that they be answered by others—leaders in local and state

> *I now believe that what makes it so difficult to lead teacher unions forward in reform is internal to the unions' own operations.*

affiliates, rank-and-file members who want more of their careers than the status quo has to offer, and thought leaders outside the union who, like me, believe that we will not see real improvement in our schools until the unions change, especially at the state and local level. Too much of today's debate about teacher unions and reform policy is shallow and rancorous. So I offer these questions with the intention of opening a broader and more thoughtful discussion about the design of teacher unions. If we—union leaders, thought and policy leaders, and, ultimately, the union members who compose the vast majority of the nation's faculty—are to expect different results, we must realize a different design.

What would happen if a teacher union accepted the primary aims of the standards and accountability movement, especially improved progress toward academic performance goals by students? Any answer to this question would call on the union affiliate to establish new terms of engagement with two core issues that have already shaped a generation of federal and state policies. First, common standards can level the playing field of academic expectations. Second, measured progress toward the standards, a good thing especially for students on the wrong side of the achievement gap, can be used to inform consequential decisions about schools, students, even principals, and teachers. There are pragmatic and idealistic reasons to motivate this repositioning. The pragmatic starting point would recognize that after twenty-five years, these issues have proven durable and produced a body of state and local policies remarkable for their consistency with state and local policies, even for their similarity to international policies. The policy ground has shifted, and unions are called on to do different work. A more idealistic starting point would recognize that it is the right thing to invest in the efficacy of the craft of teaching in an effort to make measurable improvement in outcomes for students.

Regardless of rationale, the consequence of this new posture would be to place a different set of pressures on the development and implementation of standards and accountability policies. The dynamic would shift from needless, predictable, and unproductive yes/no shouting, to a much-needed, thoughtful how-to discussion. And with this engagement we would enter into long-overdue talks about how to assess more fairly the performance of students, schools, and even principals and teachers with the limited measurement technologies at hand and about how to use data from those assessments to inform decisions. This move must be more than a changing of ideological spots. It must lead to a re-thinking of how the union affiliate does business, a rethinking that might be prompted by the next three questions.

What would happen if teacher unions opened their ranks to ed-ucators in all similar jobs—early childhood and adult educators, teachers in dual-enrollment programs, and even teachers in char-ter, online, and private schools? The status quo understanding of the union's membership is by and large an exclusive one, lock-ing out literally millions of teachers who ply a similar trade. My colleagues in classrooms and union halls remind me that one reason for keeping out these teachers is to protect the institu-tion of public education. Another reason, equally plausible, is to protect a way of teaching defined in the main by a specialized regulatory framework created by state statute and local policy that in many cases includes a collective bargaining agreement. A union leader motivated to right the wrong of poor working conditions, benefits, and wages will find much more wrong—poor wages and working conditions, arbitrary and capricious conditions of employment, unfair dismissals—to right outside these regulatory boundaries, even if there is still work to be done within them. This is not to say that the solution to sup-porting these colleagues and potential members is to duplicate the same laws and policies that prevail in public schools. It is to say, however, that as union leaders and members rethink their way of doing business, they might be able to improve the jobs of their less privileged colleagues on the K–12 periphery. They are not only potential members but also potential beneficiaries of the good that unions bring to a workplace.

What would happen to labor relations if the primary aim of unions was to produce measurable improvement in student outcomes? In the K–12 sector, power-sharing agreements between presumed

adversaries—in statute, local policy, or a mixture of the two—
regulate the conduct of labor relations. The same policies, reinforced by years of practice, have focused the practice of labor
relations, whether at the bargaining table, in similar meet-and-
confer settings, and even in the statehouse, on the allocation of
scarce resources: primarily money, time, and human resources. As
a consequence, decisions about the allocation of those resources
have become isolated from the broader policy aim of the K–12
sector, the improvement of student outcomes. If the two were re-
coupled—not as a rhetorical matter but as a matter of evidence—
the practice would change in fundamental ways. Successful labor
relations would be evident in closing achievement gaps, improving overall performance, and increasing rates of graduation and
postgraduate success, and local and state affiliates would be distinguished for their results. There is no reason why these measures should remain isolated from other, more traditional measures of successful labor relations, such as improving workplace
satisfaction and retention rates and gains in overall compensation. Performance measures would be shared, not just top-down,
tools employed by administrators.

*How will these new terms of engagement alter the way local and
state affiliates are organized, how they spend their dues, offer programs, and are governed?* Union affiliates have much in common
with other small and medium-sized nonprofits. Their boards
and councils establish policy. They raise revenue through the
collection of dues from their members. Revenue fluctuates, resources are limited, priorities shift, staff need to be moved from
one set of duties to another. This is the substance of an organizational structure designed to get the results they are presently getting. Unions are good at recruiting members, winning

elections, and influencing policy. They are designed to do so. They have not, however, played a leading role in the advancement of student learning or in the improvement of the teaching job, especially in peripheral portions of the sector.

To do so would call on the unions to take up some different work. Dues would be pointed in other directions. Staff expenditures may need to be reorganized. New systems of governance may replace cherished ones designed half a century ago or longer.

There is no reason why student outcome measures should remain isolated from other, more traditional measures of successful labor relations, such as improving workplace satisfaction and retention rates and gains in overall compensation.

Leadership development would emphasize new understandings of organizational success. Moreover, the capacity of unions to address these difficult questions may prove to be insufficient when left to their own devices, so new partnerships would be forged, ones that would break down parochial barriers between teacher unions and the rest of the education community. Examples of local and state affiliates that have taken up this work are scarcer than those who have tried to create new terms of engagement on the changing policy agenda. Of the few, John Grossman's daring efforts to build the Columbus (Ohio) Education Association on its own freewheeling and entrepreneurial terms, Dal and Fran Lawrence's efforts to fashion professional leadership in the Toledo (Ohio) Federation of Teachers, and the forward-thinking Consortium for Educational Change in Illinois, stand out.

How will the number of forward-thinking local and state affiliates increase from dozens to hundreds and hundreds to thousands?

In the end, the problem of improving student outcomes is a problem of creating large-scale change in a highly decentralized system. As long as the number of breakaway local and state affiliates is so small we can name them all, then the rate of improvement will always be slow and change will come only after grinding defensive clashes. One thing teacher unions promise—a promise in which I still believe—is a mass movement. I have seen such movements work countless times to build leverage at the bargaining table, to elect "friends of education," to pressure statehouses. Without a similar mass movement, achievement gaps will close slowly, dropout rates would improve only through grinding effort, schools in our most vulnerable neighborhoods would still struggle to overcome the odds that are presently against them.

Twenty-five years after I took the keys to room 106 at Martin Luther King Jr. Middle School, Randi Weingarten, the newly elected president of the American Federation of Teachers, made a powerful call to start a movement. "With the exception of vouchers, NO ISSUE should be off the table, provided it is good for children and fair to teachers." As I read it, this is a call, one offered in Alinsky's spirit of compulsive curiosity, for new terms of engagement. When she says "everything is on the table," she does not just mean bargaining tables, district boardroom tables, or the tables in the state legislature. She means tables in the schoolhouse where building reps and principals take on the incredibly hard work of getting more kids to proficiency or graduation or beyond. And she surely means tables in union halls, where leaders do their best to represent the nation's teachers. It is at all of these tables that I hope leaders will try to answer the five questions I ask above.

Weingarten is asking all of us who care about America's schools, including our teacher unions, to get out in front, to take a posture like the one Rich Rosivach proposed when he was forging progress room by room at Thomas Jefferson High. And she is not asking for a select few locals to volunteer to get out in front. She is trying to light the fuse that would propel a mass movement forward. Whether that movement begins now, or twelve months from now, it is the union movement I still believe in. There is plenty to do to make it happen. Let's get after it.

13

WHOEVER WANTED A STANDARDIZED CHILD ANYWAY?

—⚭—

Dennis Littky

I pretty much already knew in the seventh grade what I know now.

In seventh-grade social studies class, I handed in fifteen extra-credit reports to get an A. My dad worked next to a travel office and brought home travel books. I would copy a few paragraphs, draw a beautiful cover, and hand it over. I never really read what I turned in, and I'm sure my teacher didn't either—and I got an A, every time.

This was when I knew that schools were not about real learning. Learning to my teachers, and thus to the students, was a game. Learning was about handing in reports and memorizing facts. This was the same game that Ted Sizer wrote about in *Horace's Compromise: The Dilemma of the American High School*, which illuminated the deals made between students and teachers—do what I say, don't cause any trouble, and I will give you a good grade.[1] I played the game and got my A's; I knew I wasn't really learning, but I was too busy with the game to figure out what to do about it.

In eighth grade, our science teacher had us draw large posters of how things worked. I drew well, with lots of colored magic markers, and received an A for information that I had copied out of the encyclopedia. I never really understood what I copied, but I still did a fine job of it. The posters adorned the hallways and everyone raved. As an eighth grader, I knew that was not learning. I knew a few students who were excited about learning, who read books on their own, who went to museums instead of playing baseball, and who did sloppy but brilliant posters for which they received Ds. They knew what real learning was.

In high school, I was still too busy getting good grades to learn. I thought college at the University of Michigan would be different. It wasn't—but I loved the campus, the coeds, and the sports. My classes were big, and I had to work too hard to really think, to use my mind well. Only during finals would I understand a course and connect all the pieces. Again, there were a few students in my classes who earned worse grades, but some of them would read five books by an author rather than studying the one assigned book for the test. That was real learning.

During my senior year, with a professor's support, I designed and taught my own course for psychology majors. Every Tuesday night, I took twenty students to the back ward of a mental hospital where they talked to patients. In class the next day, we debriefed about our experiences, read materials to help us understand, and planned ways to make the hospital a better place. My philosophy, at twenty-one years old, was to involve the student in the real work with severe schizophrenic patients and then read, write, and talk about the experience. Finally, I was able to form my own ideas of what learning was and how to apply it so that other students and I could really begin to learn and would want to continue to learn.

Graduate school in psychology at the University of Michigan gave me the opportunity to teach a freshman psychology course—another chance to explore *what learning is,* not just read about it. As a matter of fact, that was the course's first six-week theme. I covered each of my topics of study with action first, reading second. The freshmen worked at daycare centers, mental hospitals, and research labs. They read literature connected to each topic (not textbooks), and I evaluated them based on their success in the field, their growth as a practitioner, and their integration of new knowledge into their practice.

I was planning to be a practicing psychologist. Instead, I used my PhD as a community organizer/curriculum developer in Ocean Hill Brownsville, an experimental decentralized school district in Brooklyn with about nine thousand students. I watched elementary students trying to learn to read out of a programmed instruction book. As I expected, the students could finish the book correctly but didn't learn to read. Then came my first major encounter with standardized testing. The superintendent thought tests did not show what his low-income black students knew, nor could the tests help the teachers teach the child. In protest, the superintendent refused to give the tests to the students and turned the tests back to the central office with all the answers filled out correctly by his staff. He asked a colleague and me to develop a diagnostic test that could be given

> *As I expected, the students could finish the instruction book correctly but didn't learn to read.*

individually. We developed the test, trained the parents working in the school to administer it, and provided feedback to the teachers about the students' learning. We did further testing every three months as a better way to look at growth than a once-a-year standardized test.

As an impressionable twenty-five-year old, I realized that standardized tests measured only one limited aspect of each student's learning. Forty years later, in my book *The Big Picture*, I quoted Kenneth Wesson, a founding member of the Association of Black Psychologists: "Let's be honest, if poor inner-city children consistently outscored children from wealthy suburban homes on standardized tests, is anyone naïve enough to believe that we would still insist on using these tests as indicators of success?"[2] Since my time in Ocean Hill Brownsville, I have fought to prevent standardized tests from defining *what learning is*.

As I moved on and became a young professor of education at Stony Brook University in New York, I had strong views on what I thought education needed to be. I am now embarrassed to recall how I thought I knew it all and how the older professors must have viewed me. Yes, I had the theory; but I was just at the beginning of filling out the details and understanding it in a deep way. I had my college students start work immediately in a public school, simultaneously giving the teachers at the school graduate credit for our study. I was preparing students to become teachers by teaching, debriefing, reading, and teaching again for two years.

I then had the opportunity to combine the pieces of my philosophy in action by starting a new public middle school in a growing community. This was one of the most exciting times of my life. At age twenty-seven, I hired twenty-two new teachers and created a middle school from scratch. My overall goals for Shoreham–Wading River Middle School were informed by what I already knew in seventh grade. Every student was in an advisory. English and social studies and math and science were integrated into double periods. Teachers saw only fifty students a day. I broke the school into three two-hundred-student small schools. The best social studies project took place at a nursing home, where the students wrote a book about how to develop a curriculum around a nursing home. The students ran a health food store. Problem students had internships. We started a farm at the school that became a learning environment. The arts were emphasized with mandatory courses in pottery, metal working, stained-glass making, and woodworking. For assessment, we used narratives as well as grades based on performance outcomes. Shoreham–Wading River Middle School was acclaimed as a model for middle school and written about in Joan Lipitz's *Successful Schools for Young Adolescents.*[3]

After six intense years, I left when the school was strong and then spent three years in a small, poor rural town in the hills of New Hampshire. I did not work in education. I rebuilt a cabin, read, and developed other parts of myself in pursuit of my goal as a lifelong learner. I started a town newspaper, learning how, along with fifteen other people, by actually doing it. I came across lots of people who were very smart but not book smart. I was elected to the state legislature part-time and learned about politics by putting myself in the middle of it all. Those three years helped me look at learning in a broader, nonschool way. As my money ran out, I applied for the principalship of Thayer Junior/Senior High School, the town's only postelementary school. I got the job and started to understand what a failing school really was, back before the federal government popularized the term.

The school had high dropout and absentee rates and low college attendance rates. It was not a place where a whole lot of learning was going on, although the staff members tried their best. I started during the summer by meeting with every one of the three hundred students individually to listen to them and plan together. *One student at a time* and *what's best for kids,* my core philosophies now, started to emerge in that summer of 1981.

The curriculum clearly did not match the interests of the students. Every learning experience was text based. I used the one teacher's salary I was given to fund three part-time positions: an internship coordinator, a parent coordinator, and a carpenter. The internship coordinator's job was to give every student an opportunity to do real work in the community. The parent coordinator was hired to involve parents as mentors and tutors and to use their own job sites for internships for our students. The carpenter involved a group in building a classroom. By paying attention to the students and making education more real and part of the community, the dropout rate declined dramatically and college attendance rates increased greatly.

Ted Sizer selected us as the first school to join the Coalition of Essential Schools, and our popularity grew. Visitors started coming from all over the country to see this little rural school. In the sixth year, the school board fired me for all the philosophical reasons I believed in—internships, advisories, and close relationships. I fought for two years and won the case locally and before the state supreme court. The story made national news: we were in *Newsweek* in 1984, Susan Kammeraad-Campbell wrote the book *Doc: The Story of Dennis Littky and His Fight for a Better School*, and NBC made the movie *A Town Torn Apart*.[4]

This notoriety gave us a renewed chance to spread the word. We created a satellite television show (yes, before there was such a thing as Skype) where we could show other schools excellent examples of advisories, internships, assessment, math instruction, and more. Funded by CVS Pharmacy and Annenberg/Corporation for Public Broadcasting, *Here, Thayer and Everywhere* went live every Monday to five hundred schools around the country. While I felt strongly that the way to make change was one school at a time, this was our attempt at scaling up the idea.

I started by meeting with every one of the three hundred students individually to listen to them and plan together. One student at a time *and* what's best for kids, *my core philosophies now, started to emerge.*

After fourteen years at Thayer, Ted Sizer invited me to the Annenberg Institute for School Reform at Brown University. Before I went, I snuck off for a six-month trip throughout third-world countries in Southeast Asia. The trip actually reinforced my philosophy of how people learn. As I watched parents bring up and educate their children in their communities, without schools, it all seemed so much more natural for the whole community to raise the children.

Soon after arriving at Brown with my colleague Elliot Washor, we talked with the Rhode Island Commissioner of Education about starting a school in Providence. I thought I was done running schools, but we said yes to the opportunity of truly taking our philosophy and completely redoing the structure of high school.

The 1995 design of the Met School in Providence started the next period of growth. I realized that my philosophy needed an extremely different structure to maximize learning. I felt strongly that subject matter–based curriculum, seat time, Carnegie units, and forty-five-minute classes could never produce the kind of education we truly want for our students.

The Met allowed us to create an entirely new structure and schedule for high school education. We built the school using the mantra *what's best for the kids*. Our job was to help all students find their interests and passions and match them with a job site and mentor in the community. This way of learning through interests was coordinated by an adviser/teacher who supplemented the work with the depth and tools in math, reading, and writing. Family members were included from day one as part of the learning team to guide their children as well as observe student exhibitions every nine weeks to see how their children were doing. The teacher's role was completely redesigned, allowing them the time and flexibility to excel. Free from seat time and specific classes, we assessed students' progress toward the goals set by the school and the state.

Since we have moved into the twenty-first century, the list of skills always important in my work have became more popular and easier to sell as a part of the program. In *The Global Achievement Gap*, Tony Wagner provides examples of how the real work of the Met students leads to an acquisition of specific twenty-first-century skills. In the bestselling *Drive*, Dan Pink writes about the way the Met's philosophy promotes engagement rather than compliance. Similarly, Pink's research demonstrates that students and adults need to direct their own lives as they learn and create new things. He uses the Met as an example of a place that does this.

The Met had tremendous success preparing low-income, first-generation students to be engaged in their learning—coming to school, not dropping out, and committing to college and other postsecondary programs. Through Big Picture Learning, the Met model has scaled up, spreading nationally and internationally and producing over a hundred new schools, while the original Met in Providence continues to thrive and evolve.

While I advocate this kind of scaling-up to produce change, it has become clear that policy powerfully enables or prohibits scaling-up. My personal philosophies about education have only strengthened as the evidence accrues; the lack of increase in students completing high school supports my view that tweaking around the edges is not enough. The new core curriculum and dependence on standardized tests will only make it harder to improve the schools and systems that educate our youth. I am all for accountability, but as long as we use inaccurate measures of students' growth, we will never truly improve the way we educate our youth. We measure what we value. If we believe that curiosity, moral courage, application of knowledge, and perseverance are as important as reading, writing, and speaking, then let's create schools that allow students to learn those qualities, and let us measure them.

As I watch attempt after attempt to make every student learn the same things, at the same age, in the same way, I wonder where our knowledge of how people learn and the respect for the diversity we have in the country have gone. I wish our current system could work, but it won't.

I am an optimistic man, and even with the education climate as is, with a group of colleagues at Big Picture Learning, I have set out to redefine what college is. During the past fifteen years, Big Picture Learning has redefined high school education. Now it is time to do the same for college. In partnership with Roger Williams University, we now have started College Unbound, an innovative program that uses our philosophy as a way for students to become career-ready by earning a meaningful liberal arts degree that will have value based on performance, not the prestige of university or seat time. At the same time that we are scaling up our college program, we are working hard to change policy and accreditation systems to expand the opportunities for more students to prepare themselves and succeed.

—⁂—

For forty years, I have understood when teachers were just playing school and not paying attention to students' interests and needs. I have also been able to run schools built around students' needs without much interference. That flexibility is over. New policies that emphasize standardization and testing have taken over. This new emphasis just makes me angry and feel stronger about the need for personalized, rigorous education for our students. It makes me think much more about the power of policy and the need to develop policy that gives schools the right to develop their own programs and to be held accountable for them.

My beliefs in *one student at a time,* real work in the community, and applied knowledge have gotten stronger over my career. My desire to push for changing structures to enable educational reform has also strengthened. My commitment to the importance of policy change to enable this to happen, however, is new. I call on foundations and the federal government to take the lead and step up to innovate in real and meaningful ways, not just tinker a little with what we currently have. I hope I can influence policy that will give every child a chance to succeed. I envision policies and the places of learning they produce shaped by the philosophy of *one student at a time,* whether that student be a five-year-old on the first day of kindergarten or a forty-year-old going back to school.

We cannot give in to a standardized world. Whoever wanted a standardized child anyway?

14

RETHINKING TRUST

—ᴍ—

Deborah Meier

Recently I came across a box of letters I wrote when I first started teaching in Chicago. What surprised me was that so many of the questions and dilemmas I wrote about in 1963 remain central to my thinking today—and I still don't have the answers to them! I was curious, then as now, about the impact of public education in particular on the unentitled, the least advantaged children. What would have to change, I asked, about how schools relate to their students, teachers, and communities if education is really to serve the democratic purposes that led to the invention of universal mandatory schooling?

I began my career following the premise that what was good for the wealthiest and most powerful would be best for the poorest and least powerful. It was easy to see, then as now, that many of these students sabotaged their own work and disrupted classroom life out of boredom, frustration, anger, and deep-seated distrust about the aims of those in charge. Could schools that respected the potential power of each family, community, and child change the way their students confronted the world—as actors who could make a difference instead of passive occupants of the public space?

I learned that schools could not reproduce the educational environment that the most entitled families and communities offered their children twenty-four hours a day, 365 days a year. But I was also impressed, over time, with how much impact we could have by building strong adult communities that treated children and their families as though they were entitled and as our allies and peers. Warily, cautiously, we learned to trust each other.

I learned, however, that distrust was deeper than I first recognized. The fears and anxieties I felt about my own children's schooling were minimal compared to what the families I was dealing with experienced. I'll never forget the mother who asked me at the end of the school year why I had "stolen" her five-year-old child's dime the previous fall. Even when families got to know and like their child's teacher, distrust lay close to the surface—on both sides.

Nonetheless, we knew that every child—even adolescents—had a desperate but often sleeping ally at home. If the school and extended family joined forces, we would have great power to make a change in a young person's future trajectory. The schools I worked in erred on the side of including the family, even against the advice of our students, and more often than not we were right.

But we needed more than families to be our allies. As progressive educators, we constantly came up against the limitations of the basic structure of schooling and how utterly alien it is to normal human learning. Instead we sought to immerse kids in a powerful and interesting community of adults/experts. The impact of this kind of immersion on the learning of novices is something we recognize in so many areas of life but rarely in the academic sphere. For instance, we know what a powerful impact teenage athletes have on their younger siblings, who hang out watching the big kids play, but we offer them nothing equivalent when it comes to developing the muscles that make us intellectually powerful.

To create such a community of expertise, however, we needed to be a team. This required a trusting relationship, and not just between individual students or families and individual adult teachers. It was far more efficient when the two institutions of school and family could surround kids with a place to relax, give up posturing, and let down their guard and their fear of seeming ignorant.

That undertaking turned out to be far more difficult. I discovered, to my surprise, that the adults in school—even colleagues who had more or less equal power—found it hard to trust each other. Something about teaching is so personal and raw that teachers spend a lot of energy avoiding serious help from those who could best give it. If critiquing an adult's writing or singing may seem hard, just *Something about teaching is so personal and raw that teachers spend a lot of energy avoiding serious help from those who could best give it.* having an opportunity to observe a colleague's teaching seems almost beyond reach. We asked students to expose their ignorance in the setting of their peers but feared doing so ourselves. Until we can overcome this, many of the reforms I think would work in school appear utopian. For if we cannot even trust each other as professionals, how can we expect the families and children to trust us?

Maybe we need to abandon the idea of trust as too vague and loose a term. Maybe we just need to learn how to be tough enough to accept criticism even when not perfectly worded or phrased: "So what? I'm getting a second opinion, but in the end I will have to decide how to use it."

Maybe democracy itself requires a tougher skin, and maybe schools need to be places where disagreements are embraced, treasured, and defended, not avoided. We don't have to mimic right-wing radio mean-talk, but we do have to teach each other to tolerate styles of disagreement different from ours and learn to use them toward our own ends. The same could be said for students who get occasional bad or mean teachers: maybe we need to help them figure out how they can get the most out of even difficult experiences.

Is this best done when families and teachers have a choice about the kind of school they become members of? Are the trade-offs that such choices entail worth it or not? Clearly a school community in which everyone feels like a willing member is more likely to resolve issues of trust and respect. But some say school choice divides civic communities in ways that endanger democracy. And there is truth in both perspectives. The same issues may arise around school size. While a small community can engage in far more powerful discourse, learn more about its members, and revise its practices more easily, there is also an exclusivity and narrowness that can come with smallness, especially smallness linked to choice.

These considerations also affect the value of desegregating schools by income, language, and race. There has always been something patronizing about the idea that some kinds of kids couldn't learn well without other kinds of kids being present. This is demeaning and untrue. But what remains true is that students learn from each other, and they learn from the way their world is organized. And what they learn when we separate them is dangerous, inaccurate, and surely bad for democracy.

I still think that there will be no serious changes in the schools the least advantaged students are in without far deeper changes in the way we view the qualities of a strong democratic society. As long as we see no connection between our self-interests and the self-interests of

Students learn from each other, and they learn from the way their world is organized. And what they learn when we separate them is dangerous, inaccurate, and surely bad for democracy.

those less advantaged, we will not undertake deep reform. As long as we are not outraged at the growing disparities in every important category between the most and least privileged— whether we are discussing neighborhoods, rates of imprisonment, health at birth and throughout life, longevity, housing, the legal system, access to the best lawyers, and, above all, income—we are just moving the chairs on the *Titanic*. But now I wonder if the community school is the best vehicle we have for bringing like-minded folks together to fight on behalf of their shared interest in a more egalitarian society. Maybe I have to do some rethinking about how to bring the ideals of trust and democracy together to resolve a contradiction that I had underestimated.

Small schools and small classes can help resolve issues of trust between adults and adults and between adults and kids. At the same time, they can also produce problems that make for greater polarization and balkanization. To the extent that local communities are the basic building block of democratic life, small schools organized around choice can be used to weaken the political base of democracy and undermine the larger social solidarity that we count on for democracy to work. We need to unravel these conundrums so that we can create both real intimate communities of trust and, simultaneously, rebuild larger democratic institutions that acknowledge the limitations of unconditional trust and place their faith in unconditional respect, genuine dialogue, and a more cautious, wary, and evidence-based trust.

15

"SCHOOL REFORM" IS NOT ENOUGH

—⁓—

Ron Miller

My involvement in the field of education has followed an unconventional, if not countercultural, path. I have never been a public school teacher or administrator, nor has my research focused on public school policy or practice. Since my undergraduate days, I have been concerned with broader, more holistic issues than curriculum or instruction. I have always sought to understand how the fundamental *worldview* of our civilization defines what we mean by "education" and what purposes we expect schools to serve. Setting aside commonly accepted assumptions about every facet of schooling, I have inquired into cultural understandings of human nature and human potential, core political themes across American history, and a wide range of dissident educational philosophies. After thinking about these questions for thirty years, I may now report that my perspective has changed very little. If anything, I am *more* convinced now than I was as a starry-eyed young scholar that the modernist system of schooling tends to inhibit rather than nourish the cultivation of human potential or the building of a humane, just, democratic society.

With all due respect (and a great deal of appreciation) for the progressive reformers, scholars, and professionals who have devoted their lives to the democratic ideal of an equitable and excellent system of public education, I remain convinced that schooling as we know it is an artifact of a technocratic civilization that has plundered the earth, exploited millions of people, and eroded the spiritual dimension of human existence. Asking a technocratic system to serve humane and democratic purposes is, I think, a futile endeavor. Reformers can have a modest impact on certain aspects of the system and even make a significant difference for some students, all of which is worth doing. But it is not enough, because the system as such fundamentally serves a worldview that is antithetical to humane and democratic values. I am aware that my thinking lies on the radical fringe, not only among the contributors to this volume but in relation to the entire education profession. Consider, however, that humanity is apparently entering a historical period of profound disturbance and possibly disintegration: economic collapse; climate chaos; peak oil, food, and water shortages; political and religious extremism; and other severe stresses may well represent the approaching end of the modernist era. It is possible that we on the fringe are noticing something on the horizon that demands attention.

In the 1980s, this orientation was decidedly countercultural; the 1960s had been repudiated, aggressive global capitalism was on the rise, and it was "morning in America." Only a small group of radical ecologists, systems theorists, and New Age seekers so fully questioned the predominant worldview. I do not know why I was drawn to these interpretations. I was no youthful rebel and had grown up in a comfortable, privileged environment. Yet something about the notion of untapped human potential, in the work of Carl Rogers and Abraham Maslow, spoke to me. Something about Thoreau's existential critique of emerging modernity resonated.

I plunged into studies of phenomenological psychology, Montessori education, the growing literature in holistic science (popularized, for example, by Fritjof Capra and Rupert Sheldrake) and the localist, human-scale vision found in Wendell Berry, E. F. Schumacher, and green politics. I was inspired by authors who drew fresh wisdom from spiritual traditions (Parker Palmer and Joanna Macy, to name only two), and revisited the libertarian pedagogy

It is possible that we on the fringe are noticing something on the horizon that demands attention.

of the free schoolers and deschoolers of the 1960s—John Holt, Paul Goodman, George Dennison, Ivan Illich. These views all made sense to me, and they cohered in a philosophical outlook I identified as *holistic education*. In the 1980s, despite going hard against the Reaganist grain, it seemed to me that a fundamentally different way of thinking about education, one grounded in a fundamentally different worldview, was taking root and might begin to spread.

Years later, however, this alternative understanding is still uncommon and largely invisible. True, there are now many hundreds of Montessori, Waldorf, "democratic," and other alternative schools, and many thousands of nonfundamentalist homeschoolers; some small minority of the public, inspired by holistic (or we could say "green" or "ecological") ideas, has checked out of the increasingly standardized and technocratic school system. But this is hardly a mass movement, and in the visible world of federal and state policy, universities and think tanks, popular media, corporate influence, and large foundations, the dominant themes are curriculum standards, top-down management, accountability, and relentless measurement. These are not simply different educational priorities from those held by holistic dissidents; they reflect a fundamentally different vision of education. What we do in our tiny countercultural enclaves—beginning with an earnest focus on the individuality of every child and a consequent refusal to test them to oblivion—is incomprehensible to the technocratic vision. We are, as I said, invisible.

I used to think that a holistic worldview would increasingly make sense to people concerned about deteriorating social and economic conditions, but now I think that the dominant worldview of our technocratic culture is so tenacious and powerful that it will release its hold on our awareness only when the culture seriously descends into collapse. I don't wish for the chaotic disintegration of the global economy, because that will lead to widespread dislocation, suffering, and violence. But it seems more apparent to me now that disintegration is inevitable. Because modernity has insisted on a high-consumption, high-impact lifestyle despite clear warnings that we are dangerously exceeding the ecological carrying capacity of the planet, there is going to come a crash. Our overshoot of the earth's biotic capacity cannot continue indefinitely. No modernist ideology—liberal or conservative, capitalist or socialist, technotopian or New Age—can explain away ecological realities. We will be forced to adopt a more modest lifestyle that respects environmental constraints and rhythms, that is more locally based, that is less about production and consumption and accountability to technocratic standards.

Some astute observers of this coming transition, such as Richard Heinberg, have begun referring to the emerging age as a postcarbon world. Life without cheap fossil fuel energy will be dramatically different from the world we are used to. Economic and social institutions that we take for granted will be impossible to maintain. Huge systems, including public schooling, will be replaced by local responses to local conditions. This is just what educational dissidents, particularly the libertarians of the 1960s, have advocated all along. Education, they have said, ought to be an *organic* relationship between the mature and the young, nestled in a vibrant community and the ecology of a particular place. Abstract, totalizing concepts such as curriculum, standards, and accountability are profoundly anti-organic. They replace a living, human-scale pedagogy with schooling that serves the interests of empire. We can try to bend an imperial system to serve democratic purposes, but, as we have rather clearly seen for the last 150 years, we will usually fail. We can replace a racist curriculum with an antiracist one, but it is still a curriculum, imposed by absentee policy makers. We can try to achieve equity by raising standards for every school across every social class, but they are still standards, enforced through technocratic measurement and management.

Educational dissidents as far back as Emerson, Alcott, and Thoreau have warned us about the dangers of imperial schooling; the Transcendentalists had concerns about Horace Mann's new system, which was, after all, influenced by the militaristic state of Prussia. In this age of voracious industrialism, dissident voices have been marginalized and dismissed. However, as we begin to realize that the empire is not sustainable, the visions of these various romantics and radicals sound increasingly prophetic and wise. A more organic education is not only morally and existentially preferable to technocratic schooling, in a relocalized world it will become essential.

These are the kinds of insights that emerge when one steps back from the consensus trance of the dominant worldview and examines its basic assumptions from a fresh perspective. Instead of reifying curriculum and taking its existence for granted, we can ask whether a preformed, mandated program of studies truly serves authentic learning, human development, or democracy. Rather than assuming that schools must be accountable to politicians, bureaucrats, and business leaders, we can ask why they should not be accountable to, and controlled by, the educators, parents, and young people who are actually involved in the daily rhythms of teaching and learning.

To conventional thinking, these are wildly radical assertions outside the bounds of professional discourse. Nevertheless, over the last thirty years, I have visited dozens of alternative schools and talked with hundreds of families and holistic educators, and I have seen that education can be practiced organically with very positive results. Young people discover their callings and passions, they gain self-awareness and self-mastery, and they pursue learning diligently. In caring and respectful learning communities, young people are comfortable and confident around adults and supportive of each other. In other words, we don't need to standardize and manage their learning in order to support their development into competent, socially engaged citizens. We can place more trust in the inherent human tendencies to learn, to seek understanding and connection. An organic education is one that trusts the inherent developmental wisdom of life. This is the root of its radical departure from the managerial worldview of technocratic empire.

I realize, of course, that public education must contend with an avalanche of intractable difficulties—including poverty, racism, substance abuse, gang violence,

> *An organic education is one that trusts the inherent developmental wisdom of life. This is the root of its radical departure from the managerial worldview of technocratic empire.*

cultural and linguistic diversity, and differently abled learners—that the cozy islands of alternative schools and homeschooling networks are generally privileged to avoid. I am not suggesting that a public, democratic commitment to serving all youth, even in the most challenging circumstances, be replaced by a balkanized and elitist system of self-serving private schools. I propose, instead, that we combine the great democratic principles of human rights and equal opportunity with the organic principles of respect for individuality and natural human development into a concept of *educational rights* that includes both access and freedom, social responsibility, and recognition of the unique interior life of every individual. I do not claim that an organic education is a panacea for complex, entrenched social problems or the most troubling aspects of the human condition, only that a caring, respectful, individualized learning environment might prove to be more liberating than a tightly controlled, managed, authoritarian system. It is worth noting that both Montessori and Waldorf education originated not in exclusive suburban enclaves but as conscientious responses to the difficulties of impoverished and working-class communities.

In the postcarbon world, I envision a localized public education that provides diverse learning opportunities to all without the deadening burden of mechanical accountability or standardization. In the early part of my career, I used to think that the gradual historical march toward democracy and human rights would naturally lead toward this model. Now, however, after witnessing the march of global capitalism and consumerism toward ecological exhaustion, I think that the tiny experiments in educational democracy scattered across the landscape are the seedlings of a new local culture that will sprout amid the ruins of empire.

16

CRITICAL HOPE, IN
SPITE OF IT ALL

—ɯ—

Sonia Nieto

As a novice teacher, I used to think I could change the world—or at least my students' worlds. Like them, I had been raised in relative poverty in Brooklyn. As the daughter of immigrant Puerto Ricans in New York City, similar to many of them, I had spoken Spanish as my first language, learning English only when I started school in first grade. During my elementary and secondary education, I had some great teachers, some mediocre teachers, and some poor teachers, but I always understood the significance of getting an education. I studied hard and learned my lessons well, including learning to read very soon after beginning school, and I vowed to be a teacher so that I could expand my own students' horizons.

Reading, and schooling in general, did just that for me, opening up worlds I would never have experienced in our fifth-floor tenement apartment in a corner of Brooklyn that was an entry point for immigrants from around the world. I read everything I could get my hands on, at each visit to the Brooklyn Public Library checking out six books, the maximum number allowed. This is what I wanted for my own students: an education that would enlighten, inspire, and transform their lives. So, in 1966, armed with a bunch of courses in methods and philosophy of education, a student teaching experience in a mostly white middle-class neighborhood, a degree in elementary education, and certification in the New York City Public Schools, I began my teaching career in an intermediate school in an impoverished community in Brooklyn.

It became clear to me rather quickly that I was facing greater challenges than I had expected. Not only was the turnover of teachers in my school deplorably high at 50 percent, but student mobility was also a problem. Many teachers were disenchanted and tired, and some were outwardly racist and dismissive of their students; most administrators seemed to be waiting for the day they could retire; and most of the students were unmotivated and alienated. My students, all African American and Puerto Rican, lived in poverty, many in unfair and dire circumstances. One of my best students became pregnant at fourteen and quit school; another, at sixteen, was a pimp. Classes were overcrowded and chaotic, not only for many of us who were novices but for a good number of veteran teachers as well. In spite of the fact that I loved my students and that many of them were capable and smart, I became disheartened.

I started out believing that I could change the world, but I soon learned that forces beyond my control made it impossible for me, or for anyone working in isolation, to do much of anything. I believe I became a better teacher in the two years I was in that school, learning some useful strategies, developing more self-confidence, and forging deep connections with

128

my students. I also believe I had a positive impact on some of my students, although I saw even then that it was not enough. I began to understand that structural inequality, brutal poverty, unrelenting racism, and other limiting ideologies, as well as unjust policies and practices in schools and in society in general, had as much or even more to do with my students' learning than what I could accomplish in the classroom.

Two years after I began teaching in the intermediate school in Brooklyn, a call went out for bilingual teachers to staff a new, experimental elementary school in the Bronx. Named P.S. 25, the Bilingual School, it was to become the first public school in the Northeast, and only the second in the nation, to use students' native languages in instruction while at the same time teaching them English. Finding bilingual teachers in New York City in 1968 was not easy; in fact, in the two years I had been in the system (and as a former student in that system), I had never met any teacher besides me who was either Hispanic or fluent in Spanish. Of the 55,000 public school teachers in the city at the time, P.S. 25 was able to find and recruit about thirty of us as bilingual teachers. Approximately half were Hispanic; the others were whites and African Americans who were fluent in Spanish. After my experience at the intermediate school, I realized that my goal of changing the world was both naive and unrealistic, but soon after beginning my tenure at the Bilingual School, my ideas about what was possible began to shift again.

I used to think that, as a teacher, I had to leave my culture and identity at the door.

I used to think—as I had learned both through my own experience as a student in New York City's public schools and later in my teacher education classes in college—that, as a teacher,

I had to leave my culture and identity at the door. I had been taught that these were peripheral to the teaching and learning experience, that they had nothing to do with intelligence or merit. As a child, my teachers made it clear to me that speaking Spanish was a problem, and this idea was reinforced in my teacher preparation. But after being at the Bilingual School for just a short time, I began to believe that language, culture, race, and ethnicity, both instructors' and students,' are inextricably tied to teaching, whether we admit it or not.

The Bilingual School was a place where language and culture were not only made visible but were also affirmed and celebrated. It was a place where one could feel proud of speaking Spanish, something I had never before experienced except in the company of my family and close friends. It was a place where nobody made excuses about being Puerto Rican or Panamanian or Dominican and where teachers used students' histories and realities as one important source for the curriculum. Just a few short months after being at the Bilingual School, I began to think, and I continue to believe, that when teachers affirm their students' identities rather than view them as problems, they give students the powerful message that they are capable learners worthy of an education. At the same time, I learned that when teachers bring their entire selves into the classroom, including their identities, they are being both true to themselves and honest with their students.

I used to think that parents were, if not tangential to student learning, at least not very central to it. After all, my own experience seemed to confirm this truth. My parents never set foot in my schools when I was a kid, except on Open School Night, and even then it was only my mother who ventured out. As an immigrant unsure of her English (although she spoke it quite well, having learned it throughout her schooling in Puerto Rico), she found these trips to the school uncomfortable. In addition, given her limited education (she left school in her sophomore year of high school), school was not a very welcoming place for her. My father, who had to quit school in the fourth grade to work on a farm and help support his family, found school to be an even more unpleasant place. By the time my sister and I were in the upper elementary grades, my parents could do little to help us with homework, and baking cookies for the ubiquitous bake sale was not in their repertoire. In all these ways, the school's expectations of my family's contributions were not met. I figured that if I could succeed without their involvement, then anybody could.

What I did not realize then was that my parents were indeed involved in our learning, although perhaps not in the usual ways expected or sanctioned by schools. Even though they could not help us with it, they made sure that we did our homework, and they always reminded us how important it was for us to get an education so that our lives might be easier than theirs. They redefined what it meant for parents to be involved in their children's education, but I did not realize this until I was an adult and, in fact, until I began teaching at the Bilingual School.

Parents were an essential part of the Bilingual School. They took part in hiring new teachers and in setting the overall climate of inclusion and advocacy in the school. Outreach efforts on the part of teachers and administrators were frequent and consistent. For example, teachers were encouraged to meet their students' families and to make home visits. Administrators had an open door policy. There was even a parent resource room that was located, intentionally, right next to the principal's office. There, family members—mothers mostly, but a few fathers and always younger siblings as well as grandmothers and others—attended workshops, learned crafts, spoke with teachers and administrators, and ate lunch, among other activities.

As a teacher, I was expected to engage in family outreach, and I learned to do so with enthusiasm. I visited my students' homes, where I was always treated like an honored guest. I communicated with families through phone calls and letters as well, and I invited family members to my room and to their children's exhibits and performances. I immediately noticed a difference both in students' attitudes and in families' acceptance and respect. After a couple of months, I was firmly convinced that parent involvement was indispensable to student learning. I learned to respect all sorts of involvement, from traditional PTA membership to classroom visits to the quiet but effective ways of my own parents. I used to think that parent involvement was something that could be expected only of middle-class families. Now I think that encouraging family involvement is especially significant for families who are disenfranchised and, in far too many cases, dismissed as unimportant and incompetent.

I decided to pursue doctoral studies because I had become a teacher educator before I had a doctorate and had fallen in love with the work. I was a college instructor in a teacher education program for three years before beginning my doctoral studies and then for twenty-five years after completing them. In my doctoral studies, I learned that our society's structural inequality made it almost impossible for students of color and students living in poverty to get a fair shake in education. The research of Sam Bowles and Herb Gintis (two of my professors), as well as the theories of Martin Carnoy and Joel Spring, among others, reinforced this idea. These scholars and others made invaluable contributions to education by disallowing the pie-in-the-sky myths about education being the great equalizer.[1] These theories were powerful and, given my experience as a teacher, they made a great deal of sense to me. Even though I had "made it" because of education, I knew that I was in a small minority among my Puerto Rican peers. Although I had not given up on education, I thought that, given the limitations in our society, what teachers could do was partial at best. I was not despondent, but I was certainly not the optimist I had been when I began my teaching career.

And then I read Paulo Freire. Through *Pedagogy of the Oppressed* and other books, he introduced me to the idea of critical hope.[2] Freire's hope was based not on platitudes and myths but instead grounded in a vision of social justice and struggle. His hope was about standing up *with,* not *for,* those who are most powerless in society and working with them to create change. It was a vision of teachers not as missionaries or saviors but as guides and supporters. Most of all, Freire's vision for education rejected hubris and domestication, extolling instead humility and liberation. That was more than thirty years ago, and it is a vision that I carry with me to this day.

> *Freire's hope was about standing up* with, *not* for, *those who are most powerless in society and working with them to create change.*

My belief in teachers is stronger than ever because I have seen the best of them do unbelievable work in sometimes harsh circumstances. So, while life takes many turns, somehow I'm back to where I started so many years ago. I still think that teachers can change their students' worlds, although not with the naïveté that I once had. I like to think that now I face these questions with a lot more experience and a bit more wisdom.

17

TURNING AROUND ON
TURNAROUNDS

—ⁿ—

Charles M. Payne

Over the course of three or four years, I have gone from dismissing the idea of school turnarounds, especially at the high school level, to thinking that there might really be a "there" there if we can prevent the idea from being hijacked and reduced to its simplest terms. The terms in which I initially heard it framed were hard to take seriously—just back up the truck and fire everybody. It sounded like the silver bullet du jour.

Even in its less thoughtful renditions, we should, of course, respect the sense of urgency underlying the turnaround discussion. We should respect the awareness of the corrosive power of dysfunctional school cultures that shapes some of the thinking around turnarounds. That said, my own initial reaction was that turnaround advocates were a bit naive about the complexity of urban school change; the idea that real change requires real time had become an article of faith with me. It seemed to me then—and now—that equating cultural change with changing the faculty ignores the fact that problematic professional culture is partly a function of the school *district,* partly a function of weak preprofessional preparation; it is not just a problem of individual schools. Fire all the teachers if you want, but the ones you hire may have some of the same issues as the ones you let go. The turnaround notion seemed to be yet more rhetoric of the Big, Bold, and Dramatic variety that has considerably dumbed down the national discussion of the last decade. Learning that the University of Virginia had created a program to certify turnaround specialists only confirmed my fears. So now, American universities, which collectively have shown little capacity to prepare teachers or principals for urban schools, are moving into the turnaround business. Saints preserve us! Beyond that, at the local level, my pessimism was fully justified by the ham-handed way the early turnarounds in Chicago were implemented. I have heard school leaders and community leaders there say that they learned their school was being turned around when they read it in the *Sun-Times.* That's the kind of public relations that can kill even the best ideas.

Watching how the turnaround idea has actually played out in Chicago, however, has me wondering. They seem to be accomplishing more than I had expected. Chicago actually has two parallel turnaround efforts going on. One is housed inside Chicago Public Schools (CPS). The other is led by an external partner of CPS, the Academy for Urban School Leadership (AUSL). AUSL has the advantage of having begun as a teacher training program, and, to this point, many of the teachers it hires are teachers it has trained (which may have to change as the program expands). Many observers also think AUSL has made more progress toward the development of systematic curricular and pedagogical supports for teachers. There are "issues" between the groups, but whether they amount to more than friendly rivalry is an open question. My own contacts with turnarounds have been frequent but informal—conversations with faculty, staff, and students; a few visits to school; reports from former students who now work for turnarounds; conversations with people who have leadership roles in turnaround organizations. I sit on the community advisory committee for one turnaround. Based on what's visible from my perch, I'm convinced that some of the city's worst, most dangerous high schools are beginning to show signs of doing better by their students: dramatic reductions in serious crimes, significant improvements in attendance (20 to 30 percent in a year), significant improvement on track rates. The record on test scores has been spotty, but in 2010 turnarounds across the city averaged a 10 percent increase in the number of students meeting or exceeding state standards, compared to a 2 percent gain for the city as a whole. That impresses me less, though, than the fact that I have spoken to a number of students who were bitterly opposed to turnaround when it was first dumped on them who came to feel that turnaround was the most positive thing that happened to them during their high school careers. I don't discount the stories of various forms of what some would call "cheating"—aggressive removal of the most disruptive students, recruiting better students, massaging the numbers. I am quite sure that some of that goes on. I am just saying that after making as much allowance for that, these schools still seem to be healthier places, literally and figuratively, for most students.

> *I have spoken to a number of students who were bitterly opposed to turnaround when it was first dumped on them who came to feel that turnaround was the most positive thing that happened to them during their high school careers.*

Chicago's turnarounds have been bringing in 90 to 95 percent new faculty, but it is far from clear whether that accounts for such changes as have occurred. My list of the factors that seem to matter would include:

Money. Turnarounds get 25 to 35 percent more money than other Chicago high schools for five years (and my guess is that 50 percent more would be closer to the need).

Social supports for children. Much of the extra funding goes into social support job categories that are only rumors or memories in other high schools: on-track counselors, ninth-grade counselors, transition counselors, social workers, attendance officers.

Curriculum. Academically, these schools seem to be developing much more coherent and aligned curricula. Teachers know more about what their colleagues are teaching, and administrators monitor instruction more closely than in ordinary schools. This is probably particularly true in the AUSL schools. Since they train most of their own teachers, people start off with a similar set of routines, a common language, shared pedagogical approaches.

Strong, persistent leadership. As much as I have disagreed with some of them on some points, many of the leaders of the turnaround effort in Chicago impress me as thoughtful and self-critical, mission-driven people capable of learning from their own mistakes. At Harper High School, one of the most violent schools in the city, when students returned for the first year of turnaround and found that "their" teachers had mostly been removed, they got good and mad, and some of them made the new staff pay for taking the jobs of the teachers they knew. If nothing else, they gave the leadership in the school a whole new appreciation for the importance of creating social capital to replace some of what turnaround was taking away. The following year, when they went into Fenger High—a school recently made infamous by the tragic beating of one of its students, Derrion Albert—they got a group of students involved in the process of interviewing prospective teachers so that at least some students would have a sense of connection and investment in at least some of the new faculty. I have no idea how well it worked, but it suggests a capacity among leadership, rare in dysfunctional systems, to recognize mistakes and correct them.

When people think of turnarounds at the national level, these issues seem to get lost. At the same time, Chicago turnarounds raise plenty of serious concerns. For one thing, I don't think we can say yet whether they are sustainable. That's partly a matter of whether or not the public is willing to continue to support the extensive funding that seems to be necessary. Even more immediately, it is clear that jobs in turnaround schools are burnout jobs. They put enormous pressure on staff and expect staff to put in very long hours. Some of the best young people I know, some of the most talented and dedicated, feel they can only do this kind of work

Chicago turnarounds raise plenty of serious concerns. For one thing, I don't think we can say yet whether they are sustainable.

for a few years. The kind of pressure is too often associated with an atmosphere of continual threat for teachers, as in, "You know, if things don't get better, you will be gone." Teachers live under the sword of Damocles. Accountability is essential, but many turnarounds don't seem to have figured out how to balance accountability and support.

Another indication of that is the frequency with which teachers describe their supervisors as forever shifting priorities. Today it's drop everything and do so-and-so. Tomorrow so-and-so will be forgotten and everybody will be told most urgently to put all effort into such-and-such. Much is urgent, little is sustained. The issue of freewheeling suspensions of students is a real one. I'm pretty much resigned to the idea that in long-out-of-control schools, leadership has first got to take control, and suspensions are a part of that. That recognized, I'm not sure there has been enough thinking about alternative ways to handle the most persistently disruptive students or about how to best support the students while they are suspended.

Right now, it seems the best thing we can say is that turn-arounds leave us with a bunch of intriguing maybe's. Maybe if you provide more resources, maybe if you invest heavily in social supports for students, maybe if you institutionalize higher expectations for behavior and instruction, maybe if we select leadership and faculty more carefully—then, maybe, meaningful changes, even meaningful change at scale, don't always have to take forever.

Given what is at stake, we have to be keep ourselves open to the possibilities. The right question to bring to the turnaround discussion isn't whether it is a good idea or a bad one; the better question is, *What would it take for us to make something out of it?* One thing that is definite in the face of rapidly scaling up something we only dimly understand is that keeping an open mind toward turnarounds will be increasingly difficult. With so much money on the table, there will be no shortage of people who have all the answers.

18

AGAINST THE GRAIN

—ɯ—

Larry Rosenstock

I used to think that traditional public education was the institution with the most promise for developing social equality in the United States.

I first taught when I became a carpentry teacher for inner-city students at the height of the desegregation struggles in the 1970s in Boston. At the time, I thought that traditional public education was the best vehicle for rising out of social disadvantage and for solving some of the most egregious forms of segregation by class and race. Having just been in law school, I realized the very first day of teaching these working-class kids (who affectionately called themselves "knuckleheads") that they were every bit as bright as the middle-class "kids" I was just with in law school. This realization has driven my work ever since. I thought we could provide these Boston students the same outcomes as the middle-class law school students if only we could engage their natural intelligence, develop their skills, and help them set their sights higher.

As a union building representative and member of my local's executive committee, I used to think that collective bargaining could empower us to become better teachers and transform our schools.

As a former tenant organizer, I thought that elected school boards were an important part of local democracy, giving voice to low-income and unrepresented parents and community members. I thought local school boards could be an effective vehicle for democratic participation in, and transformation of, the precious institution of public schooling.

And then I saw that public schools were part and parcel of the social injustice I was hoping to change. At best, our schools perpetuated race and class inequality, and at worst, they promoted it by tracking students by "ability" and "vocation," labels that, in truth, were proxies for their skin color and the education level of their parents. Even in schools that were diverse as a whole (which were becoming fewer and fewer), once inside the school doors, students of different races and class backgrounds had profoundly segregated experiences. The lawyers' and professors' sons and daughters took the honors and AP classes, while the working-class kids came to me in "voc ed."

I saw that teacher unions, administrators, parents, and school boards were locked in a bureaucratic stasis of self-interest. It is a dysfunctional stasis, yet in perfect equilibrium, and is therefore very difficult to dislodge. The unions had chosen to pull up the ladder—protect those with the most seniority without regard to commitment, creativity, teaching ability, or any of a host of other values that are more important to children's happiness and learning. The union also defined its role as the defender of job security for any and all teachers, regardless of whether they were detrimental to students or otherwise ill-suited to teaching.

I saw that teachers who were used to teaching a narrow band of students—either the AP or remedial stripe—were not interested in stretching themselves to teach fully integrated groups of students who would require a widely differentiated curriculum. Even in our own progressive charter middle and high schools, which purportedly attract students because of their diversity and alternative pedagogy, we experience pressure from parents to separate out the advanced students. At one point early in our history, some of our teachers wanted to break out math classes into several tracks. We projected out what would happen to class groupings and schedules and realized we would soon have our own internally segregated schools if we took that path. So we did not, and still do not, segregate students—at all.

In my first month as a school principal in a large traditional urban high school, a school board member tried to muscle me into filling my first new teacher hire with one of his friends. I resisted, as hiring competent teachers is one of a principal's most important tasks. That school board member then proceeded to try to block everything, large and small, that I had before the school board. I think that experience is not an isolated one, and many school board members use their role as patronage vehicles. Elected school boards are rare in most industrialized countries and present an odd combination in this one. They offer an illusion of democratic participation but do not really provide it. They are very rarely able to generate substantial reform but are able to prevent it. What they can do is control minutia and thus often become absorbed in micromanagement.

Now I see that my dreams about public education can indeed come true—if schools, teachers, and students are able to break out of the bureaucratic constraints that are smothering most public schools. There are small, integrated schools all over the country—many of them are charter schools, others are within districts—that have negotiated the freedoms necessary to hire their own teachers and empower them to be cocreators of schools.

I have visited many schools in many states over the last three decades. I almost universally find that in small, independent schools, whether privates, pilots, or public charters, the teachers have far more control of their work than teachers do under collective bargaining agreements.

I have seen more authentic assessment in such schools than in traditional district schools. I have been to evening exhibitions of student work in these schools where the building is packed with parents, grandparents, siblings, and cousins because the students have told them all, "You must come see what I did." This is a form of transparency of what students and teachers are up to that gives new meaning to public participation. This is a different way to have strong community engagement—inviting the community into schools on a regular basis to see students present their work. Another powerful method is the internship, in which students engage in real work and real learning alongside a mentor in the community and are not isolated from the adult world they are preparing to enter.

It is possible to have choice with diversity. A nonmeritocratic, zip-code–based lottery randomly selects students in a way that ensures diversity. One can find schools that are both diverse and integrated, coupled with no ability grouping within the school.

I now work in a setting that has a graduate school of education fully immersed in our K–12 public charter schools. Adult learning is integrated with student learning in a community of learners. It involves planning and executing differentiated instruction for diverse students in an integrated setting. It is founded on an integration of "head and hand"— a marriage of the pursuit of literacy and numeracy through a constructivist, applied, expeditionary pedagogy.

Now I see that my dreams about public education can indeed come true— if schools, teachers, and students are able to break out of the bureaucratic constraints that are smothering most public schools.

Now I see K–12 schools coupled with adult graduate school learning embedded within a conceptual framework of inquiry and design, leadership, and reflective practice. This is the democratic schooling I have longed for. It can happen.

19

HIGH-STAKES PROGRESSIVE
TEACHER UNIONISM

—⁓—

Mark Simon

I taught high school for sixteen years and was president of a large National Education Association (NEA) teacher union local for another twelve years. More recently, I have been a consultant to teacher unions, promoting the idea of progressive teacher unionism. My focus has moved from students to teachers to teacher unions and then to federal policy and the world of education researchers and think tanks.

When my focus was on students, I and they were grappling with ideas as if the ideas really mattered. When my focus was on teachers, I had a clear sense of mission and a sense of a righteous cause. When my focus was on teacher unions, I became frustrated at the gap between potential and what we have been able to accomplish. Now that I'm working with researchers attempting to affect federal policy, I have begun to realize the extent to which the policy consensus is not driven by anything even close to a classroom perspective or what is best for students or teachers. My perspective has evolved, but I'm still not sure how to change the dynamic that leads to bad education policy in this country.

I used to think the goal of teacher unions was to improve pay and teacher working conditions. Now I think better pay and working conditions will likely be an indirect result of the credibility unions achieve, or don't—their contribution to helping teachers teach better, students learn better, and families be engaged in their children's education. The teacher union is the organized voice of teachers, and there is no reason that voice shouldn't be focused as much on curriculum, instruction, assessment, and evaluation issues as on pay and hours. It's an expanded agenda for the union, not a different one. The expanded agenda for the organization that represents teachers is essential if the teacher's voice is going to have the influence it needs to have.

I served twice as president of NEA's third-largest teacher union local, in Montgomery County, Maryland, once for six years beginning in 1985 and then for six years beginning in 1997. The first time I ran as a militant unionist on a platform of grassroots organizing around fairly traditional union concerns. The second time I led the union, I ran as a "new unionist" championing strategies for improving the quality of teaching, including peer review and the development of a professional growth and improved teacher evaluation system. I wasn't only motivated because the new NEA president, Bob Chase, had introduced new unionism in 1997, or because our local had been invited to join the Teacher Union Reform Network (TURN). For me, it was also a realization that if teacher union leaders weren't the ones advocating reforms that preserve the integrity of good teaching and real learning, others would step into the breach with very different ideas. The alternative would be Taylorist teacher-proofing strategies. Even in the 1990s we realized that if educators didn't step up to the plate on the tough issues, non-educators would step in advocating ideologically driven faux reforms. We underestimated the sense of self-righteousness that the mission to fix public education could bring in the new millennium.

Today, the antiteacher and antiunion reform approach has hit with such a vengeance that I think it is clear, with hindsight, that progressive union reformers, always in the minority, moved too slowly, too late, and with too little boldness. But the expanded view of the mission of the union is the right one. Teacher unions have a responsibility to advocate not just in the narrow self-interest of their dues-paying members but in the public interest, from a teacher's perspective. It is from the vantage point of our most respected and ac-complished teacher-members that unions have tremendous credibility

> *Today, the antiteacher and antiunion reform approach has hit with such a vengeance that it is clear, with hindsight, that progressive union reformers moved too slowly, too late, and with too little boldness.*

with the public and with younger teacher-members. The challenge to teacher union leadership today is to get beyond the industrial model that protects the weakest link and fits the stereotype that is perceived as part of the problem in order to adopt a more thoughtful agenda that articulates solutions of which the most respected of our members would be proud.

For example, we created a whole new governance structure in our local called Councils on Teaching and Learning. We organized teachers in each grade level and subject disciplines around issues of curriculum, instruction, and assessment in order to have an impact on district policy. Or, in another example, when we learned that the district was planning to reconstitute a low-performing school, the union jumped in with its own plan for what the intervention should look like. With hindsight, these were exactly the right things to do. We read Koppich and Kershner's *United Mind Workers* and the prescriptions of Darling-Hammond's *National Commission on Teaching and America's Future*. There was a beginning theory for what we were trying to do. I wish we had done more writing to contribute to the flowering theory.

I work these days with both the NEA and the American Federation of Teachers (AFT) trying to help teacher union locals and the national unions train and nurture progressive union leadership. It implies a different way of operating, a different way of allocating staff and resources, and a different way of talking to teachers. Rather than being against reform, the union has to become the biggest advocate of reform—but reform done right.

I also used to think that great teaching was simply a mix of enthusiasm and belief in the capabilities of my students. Now I think that the mythology that anyone can teach if you just believe that *all students can learn* may be the biggest lie undermining teaching as a profession. Of course, all children can learn at high levels under all the right conditions, but when the mantra becomes a club wielded by enemies of the teaching profession, we should be wary.

I admit that I treasured my autonomy as a teacher. We had fun in my classes, but I'm not sure I wasn't shortchanging my students. Now I think that the well-meaning, enthusiastic do-gooders, like I was, many of whom are deciding to go into teaching for a few years before they get a "real job," serve to perpetuate a mythology that devalues teaching experience, professional skill, and the knowledge base that has to be mastered.

It takes time to develop a teacher. Those with the hubris to think they can do it with blind enthusiasm are kidding themselves. It requires a high level of organization and planning, a deep knowledge of the craft, and a broad repertoire of strategies that can be brought to bear in any teaching moment with any group of students.

I've become an advocate of system supports to develop professional skills in the craft of teaching and a common language to describe the elements of good teaching so that teachers and administrators can talk about what's being tried in the classroom and whether it is succeeding or not. More than I ever knew when I taught high school social studies, teaching *is* rocket science. The biggest difference between good school systems and bad ones is the degree to which they nurture, systematically and respectfully, high-quality teaching.

Now I think that the mythology that anyone can teach if you just believe that all students can learn *may be the biggest lie undermining teaching as a profession.*

I wasn't aware of these things as a teacher. In fact, for me, the discovery of the language that had been developed by Jon Saphier of Research for Better Teaching in *The Skillful Teacher*, and similar approaches I later discovered, developed by Lauren Resnick and Ellen Moir, to help teachers and administrators describe the elements of the teaching craft, came as a personal revelation.[1]

Giving teachers a language to describe what they do also provided me with a clear understanding, for the first time, of the consequences of devaluing the craft and deprofessionalizing the work. Being hard on teachers is just the flip side of empowering teachers, which brings me back to the role of the teacher union.

There's a voice missing in the education debates in this country. But I've learned that filling that void will take more of a focus than we've managed to give it. As a teacher union president, I remember waking up each day knowing that I was going to feel useful all day long just by being in the role. Everyone wants a token teacher representative on their conference panel or their school system bureaucracy committee. You can spend your whole term in office serving on other people's committees, signing off on other people's education reform strategies, and going through the ritualized motions of collective bargaining and a caricature self-interested teacher advocacy.

I used to think that the trappings of union leadership and the voice that it conferred were enough. Now I think that it is the duty of each teacher union elected leader and each staff person to have a plan that envisions a better school system, better schools, and correctives to misdirected accountability strategies—and then to fight like the dickens for that teacher vision. And it had better be a vision that is tough on teachers. Craft unions in the nineteenth and twentieth centuries—a perfectly credible model of unionism today—were the guardians of quality control in the face of employers' tendency to try to cut corners. In education, where the decision making is complex and we're not producing widgets, craft unionism is the better model of organization.

Progressive union leadership means teacher engagement on issues ranging from improving the teacher evaluation and professional growth systems to helping new teachers get a firm foundation for successful teaching. It means asking the toughest of questions about what it will take for disadvantaged students to achieve at high levels and then talking truth to power so that no one gets away with empty rhetoric and teacher-bashing. We have to resist the temptation to circle the wagons when teacher unionism itself is under attack. To the extent that we don't know enough as individual teacher union leaders, we need to gather our allies in the research community, and even our critics, to make us smarter than we were. Whatever our terms in office, we have to organize a personal steep learning curve for ourselves and our union leader colleagues so that we're ready to meet the challenges that leadership can confer if we dare to be bold enough.

Looking back at my own career in union leadership, I now think how brief my time in office was, how brief the opportunity to use the bully pulpit to speak for teachers and to wrest control of the reform agenda in public education so that at least the policy prescriptions from the federal government do no harm. The next generation of teacher union leaders has a somewhat tougher set of issues but no less of an opportunity to reframe and fight for the progressive teacher union mission.

20

MUSINGS

—ɯɯ—

Marshall S. Smith

My reflections don't fit neatly into the proposed paradigm for this book: *I used to think . . . And now I think . . .*[1] Perhaps it is a sign of muddy thinking, but for me there is a less crisp distinction between then and now ideas. Nevertheless, I went back and reread a number of articles, chapters, and books that I contributed to or wrote over the last forty-five years. I found that I did not have epiphanies about governance, policy, or other areas of reform. And I ended up with a mixture of both skepticism and optimism about much of what I studied and tried to do. This may be because my views changed as new research became available, as the policy environment changed, and as my experiences with policy development and implementation accumulated. Hopefully, they are now a result of at least some measure of increasing wisdom.

For me, that wisdom overall adds up to the observation that though we collectively are struggling with our economy, our competiveness, and our governance, this could be a special time for education. Increasing the odds for our low-income and some minority students is a huge challenge that we talk a lot about but to date have had relatively little success. And our general level of achievement and attainment is substantially less than required of a competitive nation in the twenty-first century. Yet, even with these major problems, there is hope for substantial constructive change. We have learned a huge amount about teaching and learning, organizational improvement, and the effective use of technology in education over the past four decades. More importantly over the past two years, we have seen new evidence of a powerful and generally positive resilience in an education sector whose players are still seeking improvement despite frustration over some federal and state policies, a disastrous recession, and continuing disagreements about how to increase student learning. For many educators, the impulse is to build and move forward by acknowledging shortcomings, trying to sort out effective practices, and maintaining a persistent advocacy for thoughtful improvement. On balance, this is a tremendous plus.

My college experience was in psychology in the field most easily described as the early years of cognitive science. My first job after college was programming the first solid-state computer used in the private sector. My graduate degrees are in measurement and statistics. I have always been especially interested in language and literacy, how it is learned and taught. I have taught at three great universities, been a dean at one, and ran a research and development center at another; directed a program in education at a major foundation; and spent fifteen years in the federal government, mostly in significant policy roles in the three most recent Democratic administrations. My introduction to education policy came from Tom Pettigrew, a leading social psychologist who focused on issues of racial desegregation, and Daniel Patrick Moynihan, as well as from a deep, six-year immersion reanalyzing and writing, with a variety of brilliant colleagues, about the Coleman Report data (the Equality of Education Opportunity Survey), the Westinghouse–Ohio Head Start data, and the Head Start and Follow-Through quasi-experimental studies data.[2] I ended up impressed by the massive amount of unexplained variation in achievement results; the apparent substantial impact of family, poverty, and culture on student achievement and attainment; the lack of big effects from most technical, social, and educational interventions such as teacher merit pay, class and school size, and teacher training; the weakness of narrow and convoluted programmatic interventions like many of the programs in the Elementary and Secondary Education Act (ESEA), including Title I; and the paucity of our theories about all of these.

I became increasingly dismayed about reports and studies that were predictable.

I will consider three areas—methodology, policy, and big ideas—that are "game-changing" policies or interventions that have big effects and can travel. In each area, my views changed over time, generally incrementally, and not in an unswerving path.

My formative experiences with large-scale data framed my perspectives about some of the standard methodological approaches used in policy studies. Early in my career I became skeptical about drawing strong inferences from survey data, the validity of most education production functions—in part because the variables and models were almost always badly conceived, weakly specified, and loosely measured—and the usefulness of the percent of variance as a metric for understanding possibilities for change. I became increasingly dismayed about reports and studies that were predictable. One didn't need to read them because they were sure to match the unswerving views of those who carried them out. Somewhat later I became dubious about the conclusions of most nontheory-based studies; these included quantitative and qualitative, descriptive and inferential, experimental and nonexperimental studies where the researcher claimed to have no a priori set of ideas about what they would find. Finally, I have been greatly disappointed about the apparent lack of interest among education researchers in external validity and in the serious and systematic accumulation of knowledge. So, when I taught, I advised students to read tables and footnotes before they read the conclusions of a published study, telling them they needed to draw their own conclusions using the data, without being biased by what the authors said the data meant.

An interesting area to me is the recent movement toward theory-based explorations where the investigator is explicit about the theory or model that underlies the research or evaluation and where the researcher examines the working of the theory as well as measures the presumptive outcome(s). There is also new acknowledgment of the importance of not perceiving interventions as having rigid designs that must be faithfully executed in all settings; instead, a deep understanding of the intervention (treatment) should give us an appreciation of how it interacts with varying contexts. This requires trying things out to see if they work and, in so doing, considering how they might be adapted when the context is less than fully appropriate. Some of this work draws from the engineering "rapid development" literature that engages the researcher in improving interventions as they are implemented. This requires the researcher to take into account variations in context and employ tight and rapid feedback loops to adjust for unanticipated variation in context or to correct design faults. When replicated in a variety of settings, these methods begin to address the very serious issues of external validity and implementation of policies and other interventions.[3] The current work of the Carnegie Foundation for the Advancement of Teaching on the Statway project is one example of this methodology. The continuous improvement efforts to improve the effectiveness of the Success for All and America's Choice comprehensive school models are other examples.

—ɯ—

As for policy—it all depends on what the policy is, who controls it, and how it is implemented. I used to think that some federal and state policies were effective in addressing some problems. One couldn't be in the education policy business in the mid-1960s without believing that a few major federal programs could substantially change the education world. Many of us believed that the initial version of the Elementary and Secondary Education Act, signed into law in 1965, was quite smart—built, to some extent, on prior research and not distorted with many political compromises. In Title I, the act put substantial sums of money into the lowest-income schools for low-achieving students, and in other titles, it supported local innovation, built a research infrastructure, provided resources to create capacity in schools and in state departments of education, and required accountability through local evaluations of the outcome effects of the largest program. Not bad! It seems as though our priorities have not changed much over the past forty-five years.

But my enthusiasm waned quickly. The conclusions many of us drew from the Coleman Report data made us skeptical of the potential effectiveness of the major federal program—a skepticism that was heightened by the first national evaluations of Title I, Part A published in the late 1960s and early 1970s. Berman and McLaughlin's work in the 1970s on the implementation of other federal programs reinforced this perspective.[4] My skepticism of the effectiveness of the Basic Grants program in Title I, Part A has persisted, though I have been heavily involved in two major and successful reauthorizations of ESEA, in 1978 and in 1994.[5] In both cases, we tried to improve the effectiveness of an already complex, large grants program. This was no easy task, since it had developed a powerful constituency of supporters all through the educational world and had become an entrenched symbol of America's commitment in education to children from very low income families. Unfortunately, its value, I believe, is largely symbolic, and too many of the same problems that the program was designed to address still plague us today.

And, while the Title I, Part A basic grants program is the best-known ESEA federal program, it is accompanied by a very substantial number of other K–12 programs administered by the federal Department of Education that continue year after year with similarly dubious measurable impact. Why don't these programs work? Richard Elmore nails one fundamental reason: in the United States, at all levels of government, local, state, and federal, as in few other nations, many of the decisions about the core functions of schooling are crafted by politicians rather than by educators, and they are often driven by ideology rather than evidence.[6] This has led to an appalling lack of theory and coherence in the design of many of the programs. To make matters worse, the accompanying regulations are generally convoluted because the writers are trying to make sense of legislation that sets out poorly designed programs. Ongoing self-correction by governments above the local level is unlikely because federal and state education department staffs are primarily trained to monitor compliance rather than help improve programs. Thus, the rhetoric of intent ends up greatly exceeding impact.

The irony is that almost everyone knows these programs don't work very well.

The irony is that almost everyone knows these programs don't work very well. Every administration, whether Republican or Democratic, tries to eliminate or consolidate upwards of forty to fifty programs from the K–12 and higher education portfolios at least once in its history. Yet, every five to eight years, when these programs' reauthorizations are up, only a few changes are made. The programs march on, protected by powerful interests and congressional advocates even when the best evidence calls their value into question.[7]

Federal policies that work toward broad structural change rather than supporting marginal programmatic change appear to have had greater effects. The core elements of *Brown vs. Board*, Title IX, and the Education for All Handicapped Act (EHA) have had—and for Title IX and EHA, continue to have— very strong and positive influences on educational opportunity. In none of the three cases has implementation been perfect or even, for many, satisfactory. Yet, each of these policies changed the ground rules in the system for different populations of students in a very substantial and defensible way.

Contrast this with the core Title I, Part A basic grants program, which operates totally within the given boundaries of the system and essentially wraps a weak and not very useful regulatory structure around a substantial increase in the level of resources. The overall result is a limited positive effect on student achievement.

Ironically, beginning in 1994, the Title I program has become the home for what appears to be a positive and lasting change in education policy. Beginning in 1994, administrations have been able to use the substantial level of resources in Title I to leverage serious and systemwide change that affects all schools, not just those programs. Title I in the ESEA amendments of 1994 essentially required states to adopt content and performance standards with aligned assessments and curriculum for all of their schools. By 1999, standards were in place in almost all states, and some substantial changes in assessments, curriculum, state accountability, and professional development had occurred. A serious structural change that reached into every state and classroom was under way as a result of a threat to their Title I resources that the states took seriously, either because they wanted to or because they believed they had to, rather than as a function of the Title I programmatic activities.

Title I of the ESEA amendments of 2002 (No Child Left Behind [NCLB]) continued with the requirements for state standards, substantially increased the required number of assessments, and added to a rigid approach to accountability that was to apply to all states. These 1994 and 2002 changes to ESEA, housed in its Title I, were directed at the entire system rather than just to low-income schools, and they asked the districts and schools to turn their attention from largely focusing on inputs to, first in 1994, a balance between inputs and outcomes, and in 2002, to largely focusing on outcomes. National Assessment of Educational Progress (NAEP) results from 1994 to 2002 indicate that the 1994 amendments spurred substantial improvements in student achievement.

The rate of improvement of NAEP results has slowed since the introduction of the 2002 version of ESEA, possibly because NCLB upset the balance between process and outcomes by greatly increasing the incidence of testing and by boosting the rhetoric and reality of the importance of accountability through testing. At the same time, it wrongly reduced attention to the continuous and necessary support to teaching and learning, the central exercise of schools. Lately, with the passage of the American Recovery and Restructuring Act and its $4.3 billion competitive program known as Race to the Top (RTTT), the federal Department of Education has again leveraged changes in state policy and budget behavior, this time in return for increasing opportunities for winning large competitive grants. The approach had measurable initial impact, as many states passed new education legislation and/or altered their budget allocations prior to entering the competition in order to improve their chances of winning an RTTT grant. Moreover, the RTTT competition spurred extraordinary efforts by all competitors, winners and losers, to focus on particular systemic reform goals and to develop and begin to implement coherent long-term plans for reform—a first for many states. Some observers have challenged the department's efforts to motivate change through competitive incentives by criticizing the nature of the policy changes that it rewarded. My point here is not that the Department of Education selected the "right" policies to incentivize, but that state policies changed as a result of the initiative. This form of incentive seems to be effective and relatively inexpensive.

These experiences suggest to me a particular strategic approach for effective federal activity: highly targeted and clear goals with leveraged funding to promote systemwide opportunity and even classroom change in the future. Federal leadership could be delivered as incentives—leadership by inducement, if you will—and resources would be conditional on the adoption and implementation of a particular policy. To help support the new approach, Congress might admit that much of the over $20 billion of federal funds focused on K–12 programmatic activities at the local and state levels is poorly spent. Eliminating these programs and replacing them with resources that support comprehensive state policies, such as those in special education, and provide general support for states that have weighted per-pupil allocation formulas would target funds according to need. The new strategic tools also could, for example, stimulate and support continuous improvement practices based on data and other evidence, rather than emphasize a top-down accountability system for schools and teachers. This would go a long way toward rationalizing and improving the effectiveness of the system in many states.

The state role also might be transformed, given such changes in the federal role. With streamlined federal incentives, states would no longer have to be in the business of monitoring dozens of federal programs, a practice that provides some 75 percent of the funding of state departments of education. Instead, federal funding could help states implement state reform while at the same time allow them to retain substantial amounts of what is now compliance money. A federal and state collaboration to provide on-demand general support resources, knowledge and expertise for implementation of effective practices, and the most likely better practice reforms at the local and school levels could vastly improve the quality of education decisions at the local level.

This sort of shift could be complemented by the ongoing national effort of states to rationalize their expectations for students across state boundaries. The new Common Core Standards were created by independent national organizations using nongovernmental experts. At this point, they have been adopted by close to forty states. The common standards could arguably lead to more coherent curricula, better assessments (since each state does not need to pay for creating its own), and a marketplace that is more accessible to innovators and more likely to produce widespread change. Both the federal and state governments have a substantial stake in making these reforms work through creative and cooperative implementation efforts.

—∞—

Experiences and opportunities shape perspectives. I have moved from university to government to university to government to foundation to government over my career. I have had the privilege to study and then to try to act in government based on what I have studied. Perhaps more importantly, I have had the opportunity to interact on a peer-to-peer basis with extraordinary people who study and people who do.

As I muse about the past and present, I discover that my thinking has either been chasing the gold ring or—in an interpretation more to my favor—evolving as I have tried to more deeply understand what reforms/interventions/big ideas might be particularly effective for improving student achievement, especially the achievement of students who come from families in poverty. "Passions," "big ideas," "game breakers" all suggest certain conditions or practices that show promise of having substantial effects, effects that are robust enough to travel without being greatly altered as conditions change.

In the late 1960s, I thought that a key variable was the social class composition of the school, a variable that showed particular promise in the Coleman data. In those data, we found that low-income students achieved at a higher level when they were in schools attended predominantly by students from middle-income families. By the early 1970s, I had concluded that integration by family income was not politically viable. Yet the idea still has legs and, as education funding mechanisms change, may take hold in some places in the country.

To replace the idea of moving children, a structural reform, I shifted attention to teaching and learning in the classroom. Following the data in analyses of Head Start Planned Variation and Follow Through, I became particularly interested in the structured, didactic teaching in the early grades exemplified at the preschool and primary education levels by the Direct Instruction programs, which focused on moving students toward greater proficiency in basic reading skills and showed strong positive gains in the early grades.

My views modified as I read Basil Bernstein's work. Bernstein was a British sociologist who found that, in the London of the 1960s, there were substantial differences in language codes between children from low- and middle-income families. The students from low-income families spoke in a restricted code, while those in more advantaged families spoke in an elaborated code. The nature of the vocabulary, the use of oral language, and the sentence structure were different. The elaborated code was the code of the schools. Without it, students did not succeed.

I shifted attention to teaching and learning in the classroom.

I also studied data that indicated a drop in reading scores for low-income students when they reached the fourth grade and showed that the scores of students from low-income families dropped during the summer, while those from middle-income families stayed level or improved. Since achievement assessments in fourth and later grades measure reading comprehension more than in earlier grades, the fourth-grade drop-off seemed to be related to students' early experiences with rich oral language, vocabulary, and content of the sort used in schools. This was reinforced by observations of homes and could be conjectured to be the reason for the differences in learning over the summer.[8]

In 1974, I began to direct the reading program at the National Institute of Education (NIE) within the Department of Health, Education and Welfare and enlisted George A. Miller and Herbert Simon, both early leaders in the cognitive sciences, to help guide the program, which focused on comprehension and the importance of rich oral and written language. As our work progressed, the various influences from the data and cognitive theory coalesced and, from my perspective, argued for the need for early doses of enriched vocabulary, rich oral language experiences, more opportunities to read substantial text and be read to, and greater time in school for low-income children as some primary strategies to offset these negative effects on reading achievement.

By the mid-1970s, my own circumstances changed, and I moved to a policy position in the Carter administration. Late in the 1970s, as Title I was being reauthorized, I argued that the structure and rules of Title I that led to pull-out settings needed to be changed. It turns out that well over 50 percent of the students needing extra reading instruction were pulled out of reading class to be taught separately, often by noncertified teachers. This seemed to be due to an absurd regulatory structure that not only resulted in insufficient time for this kind of learning but placed the student with a pull-out teacher very often less well-trained than the regular teacher. Regular teachers were less engaged with these students because the setup let them off the hook; they perceived themselves to be no longer directly responsible for the reading achievement of their most needy students. So, we made the argument that in high-poverty schools, all students should have access to Title I services and that the resources from the federal program would support improvement in the entire school. This relaxation of student targeting (the students were in schools with concentrations of poor student populations anyway) meant that the personnel in the school would be able to adapt programs and general requirements to their specific needs and to the needs of the whole school. We had created a way of easing the rules and regulations for the highest-poverty schools, which, in theory, would allow them to be creatively adaptive to meet their students' needs. This Title I reform was labeled the "whole school" approach. Our arguments for it drew liberally from the findings from studies carried out earlier in the decade by a program at NIE that made the case for coherence within the schools.

This "whole school" approach was a forerunner of the Effective Schools movement, with which I became involved. In the early 1980s, while at the University of Wisconsin, Stewart

Purkey and I coauthored three journal articles that drew from many perspectives in the research literature that emphasized the need for a collaborative school culture and coherent policies that supported effective classroom practices. We also argued that districts and states needed to be coherent, pay attention to, and support whole school practices.

We came to the conclusion that the education system could not be reformed school by school—there had to be a vision about the consistent quality of education that could only be led by the states, possibly with federal support.

By the late 1980s, I had moved to Stanford and there wrote a series of articles with Jennifer O'Day that set out the theory of what we called "systemic reform" and was later called "state standards based reform." We came to the conclusion that the education system could not be reformed school by school—there simply had to be a vision about the consistent quality of education that could only be led by the states, possibly with federal support. The driving concept of this approach was alignment (or coherence), the idea that effective schools needed to have a roughly common agenda—one guided by high standards to which curriculum, assessments, and support systems would be aligned. The standards, which would set the goals for the system by defining what students should know and be able to do, would then become the driver of the alignment process and the quality benchmark against which progress could be measured.

In the early 1990s, during the Clinton administration, I had the opportunity to help draft the administration's proposal to reauthorize the ESEA, which passed in 1994 and is known as the Improving America's Schools Act. Title I of the 1994 act essentially required that all states create or adapt content and performance standards and align their assessment systems and resources around these standards.

The implementation of the state standards-based reform varied greatly by state, and for many, the implementation was slow and fraught with state and local politics. However, within six years, almost all states had their own standards and had made serious inroads in aligning the other elements. As the implementation progressed, so did my increased understanding of the need for systemic coherence formed around content and performance standards as the set of challenging goals and of the advantages of organizing teaching and learning in terms of the new framework. In those early years of standards-based reform, the testing requirements were less than half of what they are now. The accountability mechanisms were designed to support schools.

From the late 1990s until about 2005, a lot of my earlier thinking about education reform came together. Traditional approaches toward policy making through prescriptive legislation rarely works unless it alters the overall system or the constitutional opportunities of a class of students. I believe in the central importance of coherence created by challenging goals and alignment at all levels—schools, districts, states, and federal. I also recognize better now that this has to be balanced with the capacity for local adaptation and with an understanding on the part of governments that implementation is absolutely critical. We have to stop assuming that once a policy is passed, thoughtful and careful implementation will simply follow. Quality implementation takes substantial time, sometimes painful and always difficult. If we don't pay attention to this aspect of reform, our hopes to give all of our students productive opportunities to learn and to thrive in our schools will falter.

During the first decade of the new millennium, I had the opportunity to fund and promote some of these conclusions as the director of the education program at the Hewlett Foundation. In doing so, I learned more about the value of both time and focus by looking at the continuous improvement approaches of Long Beach and Singapore. Continuous improvement processes address the core issues of positive, thoughtful change at the local level. We tried to urge states to develop data systems aimed more at continuous improvement than at compliance and punitive accountability.

I also returned to my commitment to the importance of language and added to it an appreciation for the huge educational potential of technology. By 2005, the evidence was quite clear on the importance of the size of vocabulary and the experiences of children with rich oral language and a wide range of content of the sort used in schools. Without the foundation of these experiences and skills, young children find it difficult to eventually read and comprehend sophisticated text. Similarly, the evidence grew indicating that children from low-income families were much less likely than children from middle-income families to have the kinds of experiences that would enable them to develop the language skills they would need to succeed in school.

These data are powerful and compelling. Children who have not had experiences to learn and talk before school will be handicapped when it comes to school learning. They are also unlikely to receive these experiences after school, on the weekends, or on vacations. They may learn to decode by third grade—but then, without rich vocabulary and the content knowledge that goes with it, they cannot understand the texts and other readings in English, social studies, math, and science that they will face in fourth, fifth, and sixth grades. As a result, they often lose faith in themselves and give up. Remedying this problem is absolutely necessary if we as a nation are to dramatically reduce the achievement gap. This could be a "game-breaker."

Ironically, we all seem to know this yet are unwilling to make the heavy lifts it will take to do something systemic about it. We focus on shortcuts and stop-gap measures—frantically supporting middle and high school literacy programs, which may help some but generally leave many far behind. We are too often closing the barn door after the horse has bolted.

Finally, there is technology. I think I have always believed that information technology will greatly change education sometime in the future. I believe that when we look back on the coming decade, we will see it as a time when technology became our most important teaching and learning tool. In the 1970s, I had a Plato terminal on my table, which gave me access to educational material that was not surpassed in quality until the beginning of the new century. In the early 1980s and again in 2000, I published papers about the as-yet-unappreciated promises of technology in education. While I was at the Hewlett Foundation, we supported the development and adoption of Open Education Resources (OER), which include free and reusable content and tools. The free characteristic of OER dramatically changes the opportunities for access by anyone, any time, for free. The reusable characteristic enhances opportunities for adaptation to address, for example, cultural and language variation. But, whether open or commercial, I believe that we are now in the beginning stages of a huge wave that will influence all aspects of education. We find courses on the Internet that compete equally and are often substantially better than many teachers in improving student achievement, as well as extraordinary science simulations that are available openly and free, and commercial learning games and other Web-based strategies for teaching language, art, music, the sciences, mathematics, and history. Our younger generations have already embraced technology—its widespread use for learning is close behind. If we act even a little rationally over the next few years, we will be able to integrate the power and usefulness of modern technology with a coherent and challenging curriculum for all, a strong early focus on language for our youngsters who need it, and a system of adults who value learning and continuous improvement of their craft. The results could be stunning.

Notes

Introduction

1. See www.pz.harvard.edu/vt/visibleThinking_html_files/VisibleThinking1
.html.

2. Richard Elmore, "'I Used to Think . . . , and Now I Think': Reflections on the Work of School Reform," *Harvard Education Letter* 26, no. 1 (2010).

Chapter 1

1. Jean Anyon, "Adequate Social Science, Curriculum Investigations, and Theory," *Theory into Practice* 21 (1982): 34–37.

2. Ibid., 34.

3. Jean Anyon, "The Retreat of Marxism and Socialist Feminism: Postmodern and Poststructural Theories in Education," *Curriculum Inquiry* 24, no. 1 (1994): 115–133.

4. Ibid., 116.

5. Jean Anyon, "Social Class and the Hidden Curriculum of Work," *Journal of Education* 162, no. 1 (1980): 67–92; J. Anyon, "Social Class and School Knowledge," *Curriculum Inquiry* 11, no. 1 (1981): 3–42; Jean Anyon, *Ghetto Schooling: A Political Economy of Urban Educational Reform* (New York: Teachers College Press, 1997); Jean Anyon, "What Should Count as Educational Policy? Notes Toward a New Paradigm," *Harvard Educational Review* 75, no. 1, (2005): 65–88.

6. Jean Anyon, *Radical Possibilities: Public Policy, Urban Education, and a New Social Movement* (New York: Routledge, 2005).

7. Anthony Giddens, *New Rules of Sociological Method: A Positive Critique of Interpretive Sociology* (London: Hutchinson, 1976); Anthony Giddens, *A Contemporary Critique of Historical Materialism* (London: Macmillan, 1981).

8. James C. Scott, *Domination and the Arts of Resistance: Hidden Transcripts* (New Haven, CT: Yale University Press, 1992).

9. Michel Foucault, *The History of Sexuality: An Introduction,* vol. 1 (New York: Random House, 1976).

10. Ibid.

11. Jean Anyon, with Michael Dumas, Darla Linville, Kathleen Nolan, Madeline Perez, Eve Tuck, and Jen Weiss, *Theory and Educational Research: Toward Critical Social Explanation* (New York: Routledge, 2009).

Chapter 2

1. James C. Scott, *Seeing Like a State: How Certain Schemes to Improve the Human Condition Have Failed* (New Haven, CT: Yale University Press, 1998).

2. See www.annenberginstitute.org/WeDo/Mott.php to review the entire evaluation.

3. Charles Payne, *So Much Reform, So Little Change* (Cambridge, MA: Harvard Education Press, 2008).

4. Richard J. Murnane and Frank Levy, *Teaching the New Basic Skills: Principles for Educating Children to Thrive in a Changing Economy* (New York: Free Press, 1996).

5. Diane Ravitch, *The Death and Life of the Great American School System* (New York: Basic Books, 2010).

6. Robert H. Wiebe, *The Opening of American Society* (New York: Knopf, 1984), 309.

Chapter 4

1. Barack Obama, State of the Union address, January 25, 2011, www.npr.org/templates/story/story.php?storyId=123043805.

2. Larry Cuban, *How Teachers Taught: Constancy and Change in American Classrooms, 1890–1990,* 2nd ed. (New York: Teachers College Press, 1993), and *Hugging the Middle: How Teachers Teach in an Era of Testing and Accountability* (New York: Teachers College Press, 2009). Other researchers reached a similar conclusion about reform-driven structures having little influence on classroom practices. See, for example, Richard Elmore, "Structural Reform and Educational Practice," *Educational Researcher* 24 no. 9 (1995): 23–26.

Chapter 8

1. Douglas Biklen, Diane Ferguson, and Allison Ford, eds., *Schooling and Disability: Eighty-Eighth Yearbook of the National Society for the Study of Education,* part 2 (Chicago: University of Chicago Press, 1989).

2. Individuals with Disabilities Act of 2004 (Title IA Section 601.c).

3. Mary Wagner et al., "The Early Post-High-School Years for Youth with Disabilities," in *After High School: A First Look at the Postschool Experiences of Youth with Disabilities; A Report from the National Longitudinal Transition Study-2 (NLTS2)* (Menlo Park, CA: SRI International, 2005), www.nlts2.org/pdfs/afterhighschool_chp1.pdf.

4. Lauren I. Katzman and Thomas F. Hehir, *Effective Inclusive Schools* (San Francisco: Jossey Bass, forthcoming).

5. Richard F. Elmore, "Education and Federalism: Doctrinal, Functional, and Strategic Views," in *School Days, Rule Days,* ed. David L. Kirp and Donald N. Jensen (Stanford, CA: Stanford Series on Education and Public Policy, 1986), 166–185.

6. Joseph P. Shapiro, *No Pity: People with Disabilities Forging a New Civil Rights Movement* (New York: Random House, 1993).

7. Thomas Hehir, *New Directions in Special Education: Eliminating Ableism* (Cambridge, MA: Harvard Education Press, 2005).

8. Katzman and Hehir, *Effective Inclusive Schools.*

9. Wagner et al., *After High School: A First Look at the Postschool Experiences of Youth with Disabilities; A Report from the National Longitudinal Transition Study-2 (NLTS2).*

10. Diane Elizabeth Smith, "Instructional Practices for Students with Disabilities in Urban Title 1 Schools" (EdD thesis, Harvard Graduate School of Education, 2009).

11. Katzman and Hehir, *Effective Inclusive Schools.*

Chapter 11

1. Howard Gardner, "The 25th Anniversary of the Publication of Howard Gardner's *Frames of Mind: The Theory of Multiple Intelligences,*" http://pzweb.harvard.edu/pis/MIat25.pdf, 2008.

2. Ibid.

3. Jeff Howard, "You Can't Get There from Here: The Need for a New Logic in Education Reform," *Dædalus* 124, no. 4 (1995): 85–92.

4. Ronald A. Heifetz and Donald L. Laurie, "The Work of Leadership," *Harvard Business Review,* July–August 1997, 124–134.

5. Richard DuFour, Rebecca DuFour, Robert Eaker, and Gayle Karhanek, *Whatever It Takes: How Professional Communities Respond When Kids Don't Learn* (Bloomington, IN: Solution Tree, 2004), 8.

Chapter 12

1. Saul Alinsky, *Rules for Radicals* (New York, Random House, Inc. 1971), 11.

Chapter 13

1. Ted R. Sizer, *Horace's Compromise: The Dilemma of the American High School* (Boston: Houghton Mifflin, 1995).

2. Kenneth A. Wesson, "The Volvo Effect," *Education Week*, November 22, 2002, 34–36.

3. Joan Lipitz, *Successful Schools for Young Adolescents* (New Brunswick, NJ: Transaction, Inc., 1984).

4. Dennis Littky and Samantha Grabelle, *The Big Picture: Education is Everyone's Business* (Alexandria, VA: Association for Supervision and Curriculum Development, 2004).

Chapter 16

1. Famously, Bowles and Gintis had written an article that contrasted John Dewey's idealism with the reality of our public schools. Samuel Bowles and Herbert Gintis, "If John Dewey Calls, Tell Him Things Didn't Work Out," *Journal of Open Education 2* (1974): 1–17.

2. Paulo Freire, *Pedagogy of the Oppressed* (New York: Seabury Press, 1970).

Chapter 18

1. Jonathan Kozol, *Death at an Early Age* (New York: Houghton Mifflin, 1967).

2. Robert Chase, "The New Unionism: A Course for School Quality" (speech presented to the National Press Club, February 5, 1997).

3. Saul Alinsky, *Rules for Radicals* (New York: Random House, 1971), 11.

Chapter 19

1. For more information, see Lauren Resnick's Institute for Learning, http://ifl.lrdc.pitt.edu/ifl/; Ellen Moir's New Teacher Center, www .newteachercenter.org/index.php.

Chapter 20

1. Eugenia Kemble gave an early version of the text a careful reading and a ready red pencil. I thank her. I also thank the Carnegie Foundation for the Advancement of Teaching and the Spencer Foundation for their support.

2. James Coleman et al., *Equality of Educational Opportunity Report* (Washington, DC: Government Printing Office, 1965); *The Impact of Head*

Start: An Evaluation of the Effects of Head Start on Children's Cognitive and Affective Development, vols. 1 and 2 (Athens, OH: Westinghouse Learning Corporation and Ohio University, 1969; Alice M. Rivlin and P. Michael Timpane, eds., *Planned Variation in Education: Should We Give Up or Try Harder?* (Washington, DC: Brookings Institution, 1975), 184.

3. Anthony S. Bryk and Louis Gomez, *Ruminations on Reinventing an R&D Capacity for Educational Improvement,* IREPP Working Paper No. 2008-05 (Stanford, CA: Institute for Research on Education Policy and Practice, 2008).

4. Paul Berman and Milbrey Wallin McLaughlin, *Federal Programs Supporting Educational Change,* vol. 8: *Implementing and Sustaining Innovations* (Santa Monica, CA: Rand, 1978).

5. Carl F. Kaestle and Marshall S. Smith, The Federal Role in Elementary and Secondary Education, 1940–1980. *Harvard Educational Review* 52 (1982): 384–408. See comments on Title I.

6. Richard F. Elmore, "Policy Is the Problem, and Other Hard-Won Insights," in this volume.

7. This may be changing as I write. Through a bizarre appropriation process, the congress may be in the process of eliminating many of these programs.

8. See, for example, Benjamin S. Bloom, *Stability and Change in Human Characteristics* (London: Wiley, 1964).

About
the Editor

Richard F. Elmore is the Gregory R. Anrig Professor of Educational Leadership at the Harvard Graduate School of Education (HGSE), where he is faculty cochair of the Doctorate in Education Leadership Program. Prior to joining the faculty at HGSE, he taught in the College of Education at Michigan State University and in the Graduate School of Public Affairs at the University of Washington. He is a member of the National Academy of Education and a past president of the Association for Public Policy and Management, the national organization representing graduate programs in public policy and management. He has held positions in the federal government as a legislative liaison with the U.S. Congress on education policy issues and is currently director of the Consortium for Policy Research in Education. Elmore's ongoing research and clinical work focuses on building capacity for instructional improvement in low-performing schools. He spends at least a day a week in schools, working with teachers and administrators on instructional improvement. He is coauthor of *Instructional Rounds in Education: A Network Approach to Improving Teaching and Learning* (Harvard Education Press, 2009) and author of *School Reform from the Inside Out: Policy, Practice, and Performance* (Harvard Education Press, 2004).

—⚏—

EDITOR'S ACKNOWLEDGMENT

Many thanks especially to our hardworking and persistent college colleagues at Harvard Education Press, especially Caroline Chauncey, without whom the project, from its inception to its completion, could not possibly have been done.

About the Contributors

Jean Anyon is a leading critical thinker and researcher in education and one of few scholars whose work investigates political economy and urban education. Her focus has been on the confluence of race, social class, and policy. The author of *Ghetto Schooling: A Political Economy of Urban Educational Reform* (New York: Teachers College Press, 1997), *Radical Possibilities: Public Policy, Urban Education, and a New Social Movement* (New York: Routledge, 2005), *Theory and Educational Research: Toward Critical Social Explanation* (New York: Routledge, 2009), and *Marx and Education* (New York: Routledge, 2011), she is professor of social and educational policy at the Graduate Center of the City University of New York.

Ernesto J. Cortés Jr. is the regional director of the West/Southwest Industrial Areas Foundation (IAF), a nonprofit founded in Chicago by the late Saul Alinsky that works at regional and state levels to revitalize local democracies and bring change to poor and moderate-income communities. Public school reform has been another area in which Cortés has organized and supervised successful initiatives. In 1984, he launched the Alliance Schools Initiative, an innovative education initiative to engage communities in public education, whose impact has been evidenced by a substantial and sustained increase in student achievement. Cortés has been awarded several fellowships in recognition of his accomplishments in the field of community organizing and has received numerous awards for his work, including a MacArthur Foundation fellowship in 1984. He has also served on a variety of distinguished panels, commissions, and boards, including the Public Education Network, the Pew Forum for K–12 Education Reform, the Carnegie Task Force on Learning in the Primary Grades, the National Board for Progressive Teaching Standards, and the National Commission on Teaching and America's Future.

Rudy Crew served as chancellor of New York City Public Schools from 1995 to 1999 and superintendent of Miami–Dade County Public Schools from 2004 to 2008. He is currently a professor at the University of Southern California's Rossier School of Education and president of Global Partnership Schools.

Larry Cuban is Professor Emeritus of Education at Stanford University. His background in the field of education prior to becoming a professor included teaching high school social studies in inner-city schools for fourteen years, directing a teacher education program that prepared returning Peace Corps volunteers to teach in urban districts, and serving seven years as a district superintendent. He has published extensively on issues related to school reform at all levels, from primary grades through graduate school. His most recent books are *Hugging the Middle: How Teachers Teach in an Era of Testing and Accountability* (Teachers College Press, 2009), *As Good as It Gets: What School Reform Brought to Austin* (Harvard University Press, 2010), and *Against the Odds: Insights from One District's Small School Reform,* with Gary Lichtenstein, Arthur Evenchik, Martin Tombari, and Kristen Pozzoboni (Harvard Education Press, 2010).

Howard Gardner is the John H. and Elisabeth A. Hobbs Professor of Cognition and Education at Harvard University. He is also adjunct professor of psychology at Harvard University and senior director of

Harvard Project Zero. Gardner has received numerous honors, among them a MacArthur Foundation fellowship in 1981, and honorary degrees. In 2005 and 2008, he was named by *Foreign Policy* and *Prospect* magazines one of the one hundred most influential public intellectuals in the world. The author of twenty-five books translated into twenty-eight languages and several hundred articles, Gardner is best known for his theory of multiple intelligences, a critique of the notion that there exists but a single human intelligence that can be adequately assessed by standard psychometric instruments. During the past two decades, Gardner and colleagues have been involved in the design of performance-based assessments; education for understanding; the use of multiple intelligences to achieve more personalized curriculum, instruction, and pedagogy; and the quality of interdisciplinary efforts in education.

Beverly L. Hall served as superintendent of the Atlanta Public Schools from 1999 to 2011. Prior to her post in Atlanta, she was state district superintendent of the Newark Public Schools, the largest school district in the state of New Jersey. Before then, she served as deputy chancellor for instruction of the New York City Public Schools; superintendent of Community School District 27, Queens; and principal of Junior High School 113 and Public School 282, Brooklyn. Hall chairs Harvard University's Urban Superintendents Program Advisory Board, mentoring participants in the doctoral program; is a member of the board of trustees of the Carnegie Foundation for the Advancement of Teaching and the Smart Government Advisory Board of the Center for American Progress; and, in July 2010, became chair-elect of the Council of the Great City Schools, a coalition of the nation's largest urban public school systems. She has been the recipient of numerous awards and honors. In 2009, she was named the National Superintendent of the Year by the American Association of School Administrators, the country's top professional honor for a

K–12 education leader, and in 2010 she became the first K–12 school administrator to be honored with the Distinguished Public Service Award from the American Educational Research Association.

Thomas Hehir is a professor of practice at the Harvard Graduate School of Education. He served as director of the U.S. Department of Education's Office of Special Education Programs from 1993 to 1999. As director, he was responsible for federal leadership in implementing the Individuals with Disabilities Education Act (IDEA). Hehir played a leading role in developing the Clinton administration's proposal for the 1997 reauthorization of the IDEA. In 1990, he was associate superintendent for the Chicago Public Schools, where he was responsible for special education services and student support services. In this role, he implemented major changes in the special education service delivery system, enabling Chicago to reach significantly higher levels of compliance with the IDEA and resulting in the eventual removal of the U.S. Department of Education's Office for Civil Rights as overseer. Hehir served in a variety of positions in the Boston Public Schools from 1978 to 1987, including director of special education from 1983 to 1987. An advocate for children with disabilities in the education system, he has written on special education, special education in the reform movement, due process, and least restrictive environment issues. His most recent book is *New Directions in Special Education: Eliminating Ableism* (Harvard Education Press, 2005).

Jeffrey R. Henig is a professor of political science and education at Teachers College, where he also chairs the Department of Education Policy and Social Analysis, and a professor of political science at Columbia University. Among his books on education politics are *Rethinking School Choice: Limits of the Market Metaphor* (Princeton University Press, 1994); *The Color of School Reform: Race, Politics and the Challenge of Urban Education* (Princeton University Press, 1999), named the best book written on urban politics in 1999 by

186

the American Political Science Association (APSA); *Building Civic Capacity: The Politics of Reforming Urban Schools* (University Press of Kansas, 2001), named the best book written on urban politics in 2001 by the APSA; and *Between Public and Private: Politics, Governance, and the New Portfolio Models for Urban School Reform* (Harvard University Press, 2010). His recent book, *Spin Cycle: How Research Is Used in Policy Debates; The Case of Charter Schools* (Russell Sage Foundation, 2008), won American Education Research Association's Outstanding Book Award in 2010.

Frederick M. Hess is a resident scholar and director of education policy studies at the American Enterprise Institute. He pens the *Education Week* blog "Rick Hess Straight Up" and has authored influential books on education, including *The Same Thing Over and Over, Education Unbound, Common Sense School Reform, Revolution at the Margins*, and *Spinning Wheels*. His work has appeared in scholarly and popular outlets, such as *Teachers College Record, Harvard Education Review, Social Science Quarterly, Urban Affairs Review, American Politics Quarterly, Chronicle of Higher Education, Phi Delta Kappan, Educational Leadership, U.S. News and World Report, Washington Post*, and *National Review*. He has edited widely cited volumes on education philanthropy, stretching the school dollar, the impact of education research, education entrepreneurship, and No Child Left Behind. He serves as executive editor of *Education Next*, as lead faculty member for the Rice Education Entrepreneurship Program, on the review board for the Broad Prize in Urban Education, and on the boards of directors of the National Association of Charter School Authorizers, 4.0 Schools, and the American Board for the Certification of Teaching Excellence. A former high school social studies teacher, he has taught at the University of Virginia, the University of Pennsylvania, Georgetown University, Rice University, and Harvard University. He holds an MEd in teaching and curriculum, and an MA and PhD in government, from Harvard University.

Deborah Jewell-Sherman is a graduate of the Harvard Graduate School of Education's (HGSE) Urban Superintendents Program and has built a reputation as one of the most successful urban district superintendents in the country. Prior to joining the Harvard Graduate School of Education's faculty, Jewell-Sherman assumed the superintendency of the Richmond (Virginia) Public Schools in 2002 and amassed a track record of successes that culminated in her being named Virginia Superintendent of the Year 2009 by the Virginia Association of School Superintendents. During her six-year appointment as superintendent, 95 percent of Richmond's lowest-performing schools achieved full accreditation under Virginia's Standards of Learning assessments. In addition, the district improved from 18 percent to 91.7 percent of all schools meeting this standard as measured by the State Department of Education in 2008. Currently, Jewell-Sherman serves as the director of the Urban Superintendents Program and as a key faculty member for HGSE's new Doctor of Education Leadership Degree Program. In addition, she is the principal investigator for an initiative between the faculty of HGSE and the University of Johannesburg in South Africa.

Brad Jupp is a senior program adviser to Secretary of Education Arne Duncan. He is a twenty-four-year veteran of the Denver Public Schools, where he served as a middle school language arts and social studies teacher, a leader in the Denver Classroom Teachers Association, and an adviser to Superintendent Michael Bennet.

Dennis Littky has been an education innovator for forty years, starting up one hundred schools from Shoreham–Wading River Middle School to College Unbound through the design and philosophy of Big Picture Learning.

Deborah Meier is a senior scholar at New York University's Steinhardt School of Education. She is also a board member and director of New

Ventures at the Mission Hill School in Boston, director and adviser to the Forum for Democracy and Education, and on the board of the Coalition of Essential Schools. She has spent more than four decades working in public education as a teacher, writer, and public advocate. A learning theorist, Meier encourages new approaches that enhance democracy and equity in public education. In 1985, she founded Central Park East Secondary School in New York City. Between 1992 and 1996, she also served as codirector of the Coalition Campus Project, which successfully redesigned two large, failing, city high schools and created a dozen new small Coalition schools. She was an adviser to New York City's Annenberg Challenge and a senior fellow at the Annenberg Institute at Brown University from 1995 to 1997. From 1997 to 2005, she was the founder and principal of the Mission Hill School, a K–8 pilot school in the Boston Public Schools. She is on the editorial board of *Dissent* magazine, *The Nation,* and the *Harvard Education Letter.* She is a board member of Educators for Social Responsibility, the Panasonic Foundation, and a founding member of the National Board of Professional Teaching Standards and the North Dakota Study Group on Evaluation, among others. She has received numerous honorary degrees and was a recipient of a prestigious MacArthur Foundation fellowship in 1987. Among her more recent book publications are *In Schools We Trust* (Beacon Press, 2002); *Keeping School,* with Ted and Nancy Sizer (Beacon Press, 2004); and *Many Children Left Behind* (Beacon Press, 2004). Her latest book is *Playing for Keeps,* with Brenda S. Engel and Beth Taylor (Teachers College Press, 2004).

Ron Miller was involved in educational alternatives for thirty years. Originally trained as a Montessori educator, he completed his doctoral studies in the cultural and historical foundations of American education. Miller has written or edited nine books on progressive, democratic, and holistic educational approaches. He taught in the education program at Goddard College, established an independent school, and founded two journals. He served for several years as editor of the magazine *Education Revolution*. Now retired, Miller runs a bookstore in Woodstock, Vermont, but many of his writings can be found on his Web site, www.pathsoflearning.net.

Sonia Nieto, who has taught students from elementary school through doctoral studies, is Professor Emerita of Education at the University of Massachusetts, Amherst. Her research focuses on multicultural education, teacher education, and the education of Latinos, immigrants, and other students of culturally and linguistically diverse backgrounds. Her book publications include *Affirming Diversity: The Sociopolitical Context of Multicultural Education,* with Patty Bode (5th ed., 2008), *The Light in Their Eyes: Creating Multicultural Learning Communities* (2010), and *What Keeps Teachers Going?* (2003), along with three edited volumes, *Puerto Rican Students in U.S. Schools* (2000), *Why We Teach* (2005), and *Dear Paulo: Letters from Those Who Dare Teach* (2008). She serves on several regional and national advisory boards that focus on educational equity and social justice, and she has received many academic and community awards for her scholarship, teaching, and advocacy, including four honorary doctorates.

Charles M. Payne is the Frank P. Hixon Professor in the School of Social Service Administration at the University of Chicago. In 2011, he served as interim chief education officer of the Chicago Public Schools. His interests include urban education and school reform, social inequality, social change, and modern African American history. His most recent books are *So Much Reform, So Little Change* (Harvard Education Press) and a coedited anthology, *Teach Freedom: The African American Tradition of Education for Liberation.*

Larry Rosenstock, after attending law school, taught carpentry for eleven years in urban high schools in Boston and Cambridge. He served as staff attorney for two years at the Harvard Center for Law and Education and was a lecturer at the Harvard Graduate School of Education for five years. He was principal of the Rindge School of Technical Arts and of the Cambridge Rindge and Latin School, director of the federal New Urban High School Project, president of the Price Charitable Fund, founder and CEO of High Tech High in San Diego, and president of the High Tech High Graduate School of Education. Rosenstock's program CityWorks won the Ford Foundation Innovations in State and Local Government Award in 1992. He is an Ashoka Fellow and the 2010 winner of the McGraw Prize in Education.

Mark Simon works currently at the Economic Policy Institute as an education policy analyst and as national coordinator of the Mooney Institute for Teacher and Union Leadership. He taught high school social studies in Montgomery County, Maryland, for sixteen years, was elected president of the teacher union local for twelve years, and served on the NEA board of directors. He is a parent and a community activist on public schools issues in Washington, D.C. You can read his comments on two blogs: www.mitul.org and www.realeducationrefromdc@blogspot.org.

Marshall S. Smith recently retired as the U.S. Department of Education's director of international affairs and senior counselor to Secretary of Education Arne Duncan. He has served as a key adviser at the Department of Education during three administrations and was selected by *Education Week* as one of the top-ten most influential people in education policy during the decade that spanned 1995–2005. While in federal government, Smith oversaw the development and passage of several major education laws. Outside of government, Smith was at different times an associate professor at Harvard University and a professor at the University of Wisconsin–Madison

191

and Stanford University, where he was also dean of the School of Education. He was also program director for education at the William and Flora Hewlett Foundation in Menlo Park, California. A member of the National Academy of Education and former chairman of the board of the American Institutes of Research, Smith has authored publications on numerous topics, including school effectiveness and standards-based reform.